CATHOLIC CUSTOMS

Catholic Customs

A Fresh Look at Traditional Practices

Regis J. Flaherty

SERVANT
BOOKS

PUBLISHED BY ST. ANTHONY MESSENGER PRESS
CINCINNATI, OHIO

Unless otherwise noted, scripture verses are from the Revised Standard Version of the Bible, copyrighted 1946, 1952, 1971 by the Division of Christian Education of the National Council of Churches of Christ in the USA. Used by permission. Excerpts from the English translation of the Catechism of the Catholic Church for use in the United States of America copyright 1994, United States Catholic Conference, Inc. -Libreria Editrice Vaticana. Used with permission.

Published by St. Anthony Messenger Press
28 W. Liberty St.
Cincinnati, OH 45202
www.servantbooks.com

Cover design: Brian Fowler, Grand Rapids, Mich.

04 05 10 9 8 7 6 5 4 3

Printed in the United States of America
ISBN 1-56955-282-7

Library of Congress Cataloging-in-Publication Data

Flaherty, Regis J.
  Catholic customs : a fresh look at traditional practices / Regis J. Flaherty.
    p. cm.
Includes bibliographical references.
  ISBN 1-56955-282-7 (alk. paper)
  1. Catholic Church--Customs and practices. 2. Spiritual life--Catholic Church. I. Title.
  BX2350.3 .F54 2003
  282--dc21

                                                                    2002014383

This book is dedicated to
my wife and best friend, Libbie

Contents

Introduction

How do you express love beyond merely saying, "I love you"? A husband on a business trip may send a rose to his wife at home. A handmade card from a small child deeply touches the heart of a mother. Displaying a flag speaks of a special type of love that we call patriotism.

Some signs of love have become traditions for many people: sharing Thanksgiving dinner, giving gifts on Christmas, or making a birthday cake for family members. Love is often expressed in such tangible ways.

Some symbols and gestures express meaning to others. A young man understands the meaning of the heart drawn on the bottom of a letter from his girlfriend. The wave of a hand to an acquaintance needs no explanation. Signs, symbols, gestures, and other traditions are vital ways of communication that convey meaning and build relationships and understanding.

This book concerns ways of expressing love within the context and life of the Catholic Church—love between God and his people. God loves his people. Sometimes that love requires a call to repentance. Sometimes it involves the bestowing of grace to enable the Christian to live a life worthy of his or her innate God-given dignity.

God loves by feeding his people with spiritual food, by imparting wisdom and understanding, and by bestowing peace of heart. God often displays this love through the tangible. The Bible, his inspired Word, is a great gift of love. In addition, the sacraments were instituted by Christ as effective instruments for distribution of his gracious love.

As God's love is displayed through tangible ways, so also is the response of men and women. Essentially the Christian life is a response to the love of God. We can merely say: "God, I love you." But something in our very nature strives to express that love in overt ways. Our love takes form in obedience, repentance, worship, and prayer.

Additionally, Christianity is a family affair. The relationship of love between God and the individual has communal ramifications. Scripture makes it clear that we cannot love God unless we also love our neighbor. The reciprocal is also true. True love of neighbor must be based in a love of God.

Some customs and traditions in the Catholic Church express the familiar aspects of life. The Mass, for example, is a communal expression of a family love. We join with our brother, Jesus, who offers himself to his Father, our Father. The Father receives that offering of love and obedience and returns it as a meal of eternal proportion and consequence. For people who value family dinners on Thanksgiving Day, the concept is not difficult to understand.

Spirit and Matter

Men and women are unique creatures. The biblical creation story (see Gn 2:7) and modern science both tell us that we are made of common materials from the earth. We are carbon and hydrogen and other elements. When we die, our bodies decay and return to these basic elements.

In this regard, then, we are not very different from the other organic beings that range from plants to mammals. Yet we also display intellect, understanding, and the ability for abstract reasoning. We can make choices in a way that animals cannot.

We experience restlessness as if there must be more to life than the merely organic. The search for love and meaning motivates us. Works of art and music touch something within us that we suspect may reflect the Divine.

We are both spiritual and material beings. We exist on a continuum between animals and angels, neither merely mortal nor pure spirits. Our lives are a constant expression of that combination of spirit and matter.

The artist expresses creativity on canvas with oils and a brush. The lover expresses affection by a hand stroking the hair of the beloved. In a similar way, the customs and traditions of the Church are those material and physical items and expressions that find their basis in spiritual reality.

Tradition and traditions

The Catholic Church was founded by Jesus about two thousand years ago. Some Catholic traditions can be traced back for the full two thousand years. Others are of a much more recent vintage. New expressions of faith and love are even now being developed, while other traditions are falling into disuse.

When examining customs and traditions, it is important to make a distinction between the changeless and the changeable. There are aspects of the Catholic faith that have not changed in two thousand years and that will not change until Christ returns at the end of the world. These changeless realities are God-given realities. They were taught by Jesus to his disciples and passed down through the ages.

Some of these realities were recorded in the Scriptures. Others were passed on orally. Jesus did not write a book or produce a "how to" manual. He established a community of faith and entrusted his teaching to his followers. He guaranteed the transmittal of that teaching by bestowing the divine Holy Spirit on the Church as a guide and protector of the truth.

For two thousand years, then, the Church has preserved the teaching of Christ, both as written in the Scripture and as passed on orally from the apostles down through all their successors up to the present pope. This truth that has been preserved, but perhaps not explicitly written in the Bible, is called *Tradition*. The Church has guarded this Tradition for twenty centuries.

The truths contained in the Tradition are unchanging realities and must be distinguished from customs that do change and are also often called "traditions." The unchanging truths are Tradition with a capital "T" because they are a specific reality. Think of it this way: You capitalize your name because it represents a distinct and unique reality. Catholic "Tradition" deserves to be capitalized for the same reason. It refers to an essential, unchanging, unique reality. In contrast, the customs that can and do vary are traditions with a lower-case "t."

The sacraments, for example, are a part of the Tradition of the Church and were instituted by Christ. There are seven sacraments. There will never be eight, nor will there be six.

The realities expressed in the sacraments are changeless, and some of the outward expressions in the sacraments will not change. For example, water is essential in Baptism and bread is essential for the Eucharist. However, there are parts of the celebration of these sacraments that can and do change.

For example, at most baptisms of an infant the minister places a white garment on the child. It is a sign of the cleansing from sin and of new life in the Church. This gesture is a wonderful and meaningful sign of a spiritual reality, but it is a tradition with a small "t." In other words, it is not essential to the sacrament of Baptism. If someone forgets the white garment, it is not a problem. If next year the bishops and the Pope decide to eliminate that part of the ceremony, no one's faith should be shaken.

Avoiding Confusion

After the Second Vatican Council some customs were changed or eliminated. For some Catholics this change created great confusion. Primarily it was a confusion over Tradition and traditions.

For example, the ritual of the Mass was changed after Vatican II. In the Western Church Mass had been said in Latin for hundreds of years. That custom became an option with the introduction of the Mass in the vernacular. Some will remember that before Vatican II the priest would say most of the Mass facing away from the people. That was changed so that the altar began to look more like a table and the priest faced the people. (Actually, this change was a return to a custom that existed in the early Church.)

The point is that all these changes were customs that could be changed. However, the essentials of the Mass—the part that Jesus specifically instituted and entrusted to his apostles, who passed it on to their followers—did not, and will not, change.

Other traditions have also changed in recent history. For example, the Church in the United States now permits altar girls, displacing the long-standing tradition that only males would assist at the altar. Abstinence from meat on Fridays is no longer a requirement for most of the year, although the reason behind this discipline remains an important consideration for Catholics.

Other changes will occur from time to time. In fact, customs can and do vary based on culture. Various rites in the Eastern and Western Church have different customs. As the Church evangelizes in different parts of the world, differences in the changeable traditions appear. Thus in India or China the Church makes some adaptations and changes in practices that are common in the West.

Yet the essential will always remain the same. The dogma of the Assumption will not change, even if the color of the vestments that are worn on the feast of the Assumption may vary depending on the part of the world where the feast is celebrated.

This book speaks of both Tradition and traditions. So we have made a point of drawing this distinction between what is essential and what can change. This book also focuses primarily on customs that are common in the Western or Latin Church. So we should note that it may not reflect customs from other parts of the world.

Certain principles of faith are timeless while their expression is often culturally determined. To worship God and to give him due reverence, for example, is enjoined on all believers by the commandments. In Western society a genuflection is an appropriate gesture to express reverence. In the Eastern Church a bow from the waist is more appropriate.

Is one way better? No, these are customs based in the culture that express a similar reality.

Prayer, communication with God, is also necessary for all believers. But the form of prayer can vary. The variation could be cultural, but it could also vary based on temperament and personality. Some individuals will find a novena to be helpful, while others will prefer a different form of prayer.

A primary goal of this book is to provide an overview of Catholic customs and traditions and to answer some of the "why" and "how" questions that surround the externals of Catholic activity. My hope is that with understanding will also come appreciation for the value of traditions and customs. Knowledge of the meaning of various traditions and customs can have a positive impact on the lives of individuals and can be a means of building that love relationship with God.

ONE

Living a Spiritual Life

There is one day each year that each one of us can point to and say: "On this day I celebrate the anniversary of my birth." There will also be some particular day of the year on which we will die. In between these two dates will come many other events. Some may be momentous, such as marriage or the birth of a child. Other events will be more mundane, but also more regular, such as eating and sleeping. These events will impact us emotionally, mentally, and physically. There will be growth, sickness, weakness, success, and failure.

In a similar way, the Catholic Church, building upon the teaching of Christ, has identified seven sacraments that embrace our spiritual life. They deal with life and death, with the great events of life, and with ordinary needs such as food, cleansing, and growing up. Sacraments are signs of realities that usually are not discernible by the physical eye. They use ordinary gestures and materials, but they produce some extraordinary results.

Sacraments are signs, but they are also more than signs. When administered as directed by the Church, sacraments produce intended results. Now this is not some form of magic. Consider the following analogy.

I can open a door by turning the knob and pulling or pushing the door. I also can open a door by tying a piece of nylon cord to the knob and pulling on the cord from a distance. In the latter case, someone may observe the door opening and wonder at the action being accomplished without a person being immediately present. Yet such an action would not be magic. It would merely be the use of an intermediate object—such as that rope—to accomplish the task.

In a similar way, God does mighty works in men and women through the sacraments. He chooses to do those works through various channels. It was not the cord that opened the door. So also it is not the physical means that cause the results of the sacraments. Rather, it is the action of God through those means that produces results. They are tools in God's hands.

Sacraments, when validly administered, produce real results. However, the effectiveness of the sacrament on particular individuals can vary greatly. A comparison may make this point clearer.

Imagine that someone handed you a bank account passbook in your name for one million dollars. You would instantly become a millionaire! But as long as the money stayed in the bank, it wouldn't be of much value to you. Only as you drew out funds or wrote a check would that money have an effect upon your life.

In the sacraments, through the actions of Christ the individual receives unimaginable and boundless treasure. Yet the effectiveness of that gift in the life of each individual will vary on the use or non-use of the graces of the sacrament. The sacraments can be powerful forces in our spiritual lives as we "draw down" the grace that is made available to us. But if we ignore the treasure, we will continue to live as spiritual paupers.

This, then, is a brief overview of sacraments—necessary to allow us to look at some particular Catholic customs, their origin, and their meaning for each sacrament. But prior to that exploration is one more item to cover: the elements that are "essential" to each sacrament.

Certain essential items are core to the validity of the sacrament. For example, water and specific words are essential to the sacrament of Baptism. If these are omitted, the sacrament is not valid. We will discuss some of these essentials, but it is important to remember that they go beyond the category of custom to provide the very essence of the sacrament.

Other rituals, prayers, and objects are associated with each sacrament that, while not essential, have a long-standing tradition that associate them with that sacrament. They can be changed or modified over time. However, the fact that they are intimately associated with the sacrament gives them a strong identification with it.

Compare this situation to clothes on the body. Obviously, you need a body for existence. Clothes, while not an absolute necessity, do make life more livable! So some of the elements of the sacraments, while not essential, do enhance the meaning and understanding of the sacrament.

The last category we will examine includes the more peripheral elements. In keeping with our previous example, once you have been clothed, you may want to accessorize the outfit with some jewelry. The jewelry may add some interest, but it wouldn't rank as essential or necessary. We will also discuss some of these accessory items that are occasionally added to the sacraments.

A Baby and the Bath Water—Baptism

Baptism is the sacrament that births us into the kingdom of God and the life of the Church. The administration of this sacrament was mandated by Christ when he told his disciples to "go ... and make disciples of all nations, baptizing them" (Mt 28:19).

There are two essential elements to this sacrament. The first is water. (We should also keep in mind that the person administering Baptism must have the intent to baptize and must direct the action to a specific person.) The second essential element is the formulation of the words of the sacrament. The ritual must include the words "I baptize you in the name of the Father, and of the Son, and of the Holy Spirit," which must be said as the water is poured or otherwise administered.

Flowing water evokes thoughts of life and cleansing. Baptism accomplishes both in cleansing the recipient of sin and beginning in him or her a new spiritual life. Traditionally, Baptism was administered by a triple immersion of the recipient in the water while the minister of the sacrament invoked the name of the Trinity. However, the pouring of water on the forehead of the one to be baptized is also acceptable and has become the common method in Catholic tradition.

The water used in Baptism is blessed either specifically for the administration of the sacrament or at the Easter Vigil Mass each year. Easter and Baptism are intimately linked together. Easter celebrates the resurrection of Jesus—in essence, his rebirth. The baptized are also a resurrected people. They come through the water cleansed and reborn, enjoying the gift of grace and life that has been made possible through Jesus.

When adults are to be baptized, they undergo a time of education and training prior to receiving the sacrament. This preparation has been formalized in the Rite of Christian Initiation. These adult catechumens are then baptized at the Easter Vigil Mass. They normally also receive the sacraments of Confirmation and the Eucharist at the same time.

Infant Baptism

Baptism in the Catholic Church is most often associated with infants. This practice has a long tradition in the Church. Documents from as early as the second century attest to the practice of infant baptism.

Since this sacrament is the entry into salvation and the life of the Church, it is to be expected that parents would want their children to receive it. The tradition of infant baptism can even be identified in scripture. For example, when Paul's jailer in Philippi was converted, the Scripture tells us that the jailer "was baptized at once, with all his family" (Acts 16:33). It is not unreasonable to assume that his family could have included children and even infants.

Children who are baptized as infants are to learn their faith as they grow. In the Western Church, other sacraments of initiation (the Eucharist and Confirmation) are delayed until these young Catholics have been sufficiently catechized (that is, taught the faith).

Other Symbols Associated With Baptism

While water is the key physical element in Baptism, other symbols also illuminate the meaning of the sacrament. Chrism, oil blessed by the bishop, is used to anoint the person being baptized. As recorded in Scripture and history, oil has been used since ancient times to anoint royalty and priests. This anointing at Baptism symbolizes that the new Christian has become part of "a royal priesthood, a holy nation, God's own people" (1 Pt 2:9). Also, chrism reminds us of the indwelling of the Holy Spirit, who takes up residence in the newly baptized, bringing grace and gifts.

Other symbols associated with Baptism are the white garment and the baptismal candle. These are presented to the newly baptized after the formal portion of the ceremony to remind us of scriptural truths. White is a symbol of purity and cleanliness—the state of the soul of the newly baptized due to our forgiveness in Jesus. The believer is to "put on Christ" and his life.

Jesus is the "light of the world." He is our light, as symbolized by the baptismal candle, and it is he whom we receive in Baptism. The new Christian, then, is to carry that light to the world.

Sponsors

It is a long-standing tradition that the person to be baptized is to be accompanied by one or two sponsors. The sponsor must be a member of the Christian community in good standing. The sponsor both presents the candidate and acts on behalf of the entire community as witness.

As with other non-essential components of the sacrament, witnesses

are not needed in case of an emergency. Only the one to be baptized
and the minister of the sacrament are required. That minister is normally an ordained clergy member: bishop, priest, or deacon. However,
in case of need any person can act as the minister of the sacrament,
even a non-Catholic, as long as the minister intends to baptize as the
Church would intend.

A Name

One practice with a long-standing tradition is the giving of the name of
a saint or biblical character to the newly baptized. This requirement was
removed in 1983 when canon law was revised. However, the practice
still has merit. The saint whose name is chosen provides an example for
the individual to follow and can be a special heavenly intercessor.

Worthy of Celebration

Births are worth celebrating! Beyond the celebration of the sacrament
many Catholics include other traditions that focus on the importance
of Baptism and the inclusion of a new member in the community of
faith. Post-baptism parties can include family and friends. The baptismal candle can be lit on the annual anniversary of the baptism.
Baptismal vows are renewed each Easter.

Growing Up—Confirmation

Confirmation, Baptism, and the Eucharist are known as the Sacraments
of Initiation. In the Eastern tradition of the Church, these three sacraments are administered at the same time. This practice emphasizes the
unity of these sacraments. In the West, the three sacraments are
administered together for an adult who is entering the faith.

However, with infants, the common practice for Confirmation has diverged between the Eastern and Western traditions of the Church. When infants are baptized in the Western Church, Confirmation is deferred until a later date. The code of Canon Law for the Latin Church states that Confirmation should be administered "at about the age of discretion unless the conference of bishops has determined another age."[1]

At present, the U.S. Conference of Catholic Bishops has ruled that Confirmation should occur between the "age of discretion and about sixteen years of age."[2] Nonetheless, Confirmation remains intimately linked to Baptism. The *Catechism of the Catholic Church* states that "the reception of the sacrament of Confirmation is necessary for the completion of baptismal grace."[3]

The span of time between Baptism for an infant and the Confirmation of a young adult allows time for growth in the faith of the individual. Reaching an age of discretion or maturity, the previously baptized person makes the decision to be confirmed in his or her baptismal faith.

In the Latin Church "the sacrament of Confirmation is conferred through the anointing with chrism on the forehead, which is done by the laying on of the hand and through the words ... 'Be sealed with the Gift of the Holy Spirit.'"[4] These are the essential elements of this sacrament.

Chrism, oil blessed by the bishop each Holy Thursday, is an apt symbol and medium of the sacrament. Oil is a sign of abundance. It cleanses and heals. Athletes use it to limber up and prepare for competition. It also hearkens back to the oil that was used to anoint the child at Baptism.

As the minister invokes the Holy Spirit in prayer over the candidate, he places his hands on the head of the candidate. In scriptural practice, the indwelling of the Holy Spirit in an individual was accomplished by the "laying on of hands" (see, for example, Acts 8:18). The person being confirmed has already received the Holy Spirit in Baptism. Confirmation, rather than imparting the Spirit, is thus a release of the gifts and power of the Spirit in the life of the individual.

Among the effects of Confirmation is the strengthening to proclaim and defend the faith in the power of the Holy Spirit. As with all sacraments, Confirmation is effective in the dispensation of graces. However, the actualization of those graces depends upon the disposition of the recipient.

A Name and a Sponsor

Traditionally, a sponsor accompanies and presents the candidate for Confirmation. If the baptismal sponsor is available, there is value in having that person as the Confirmation sponsor. This further emphasizes the connection of Confirmation with Baptism. Nevertheless, another sponsor may be selected.

It is also tradition to select a name at Confirmation. In the past the candidate would select the name of a saint that he or she wished to emulate. Recently, candidates have been encouraged to consider using their baptismal name. This again ties the rite of Confirmation back to the sacrament of Baptism.

The Minister

In the Western Church, Confirmation takes place in a group setting, and the sacrament is administered by the bishop as the head of the local church. The bishop must determine the readiness of candidates to receive the sacrament. He receives a report from those responsible for training the candidates and often also questions the candidates to determine their preparedness. For adult converts, a priest will administer Confirmation along with Baptism at the Easter vigil. In the Eastern Church the priest is the ordinary minister of the sacrament.

A Springboard

Confirmation is the culmination of the sacrament of Baptism, an acknowledgement that the recipient has in some sense completed an initiation. It is a springboard to an adult Catholic life, the beginning of a responsible spiritual adulthood. Thus rather than an end, it is a beginning.

Nourishment for the Journey—the Eucharist

If there ever was a topic that could not be covered in a short section of a book, it is the Eucharist. So before saying something about the traditions of the Eucharist, it is important to mention what will not be said. The Eucharist is "the source and summit of the whole Christian life."[5]

The richness of the theological and spiritual aspects of this sacrament can only be appreciated by more extended study, prayer, and reflection. Therefore, if you want to begin to appreciate the Catholic understanding of the Eucharist, the bibliography at the end of this volume will provide you with some reading suggestions.

"Jesus said to them [the Jews], 'Truly, truly, I say to you, unless you eat the flesh of the Son of man and drink his blood, you have no life in you; he who eats my flesh and drinks my blood has eternal life, and I will raise him up at the last day. For my flesh is food indeed, and my blood is drink indeed'" (Jn 6:53-55). The Catholic Church takes these words of Jesus literally.

This text is one of many in the Scripture where Jesus speaks of the Eucharist. When Jesus was preparing for his redemptive death on the cross, he took the time to share a final meal with his disciples. At that meal he established the sacrament of the Eucharist with the words that are repeated at every Mass: "Jesus took bread, and blessed, and broke it, and gave it to the disciples and said, 'Take, eat; this is my body.' And he took a cup, and when he had given thanks he gave it to them, saying, 'Drink of it, all of you; for this is my blood'" (Mt 26:26-28).

This was the last meal that Jesus physically shared with his twelve disciples before his death. But in a very real sense it was the first meal that Jesus shared with his disciples because this was a unique meal. Every Eucharistic celebration is a continuation of that sharing in the upper room on the day before Jesus died on the cross. The Church continues to celebrate that meal in obedience to Jesus, who commanded his followers: "Do this in remembrance of me" (Lk 22:19).

Yet the Eucharistic celebration is not only a continuation of a meal. At that "Last Supper" Jesus connected the events in the upper room with his impending death and with God's work with the Israelites in history. The shared meal was a celebration of the Jewish Passover, a lived remembrance of the deliverance of the Jews from the oppression of Egypt.

As part of that original Passover, a spotless lamb was sacrificed and eaten by those being delivered. Jesus had accepted John the Baptist's identification of him as "the Lamb of God" (see Jn 1:29, 36). The ultimate, complete, and final sacrifice was thus Jesus, the one Lamb of God. The Lamb that was sacrificed for that new meal instituted by Christ was Jesus himself, who died upon the cross.

So each Eucharist participates in that sacrifice of Calvary. That one perfect sacrifice is forever satisfactory. Each Mass pierces time to participate in that one sacrifice of Calvary.

Thus the Eucharist is both perfect sacrifice and perfect meal. Each Mass re-enters the drama of what has come to be called the "Paschal Mystery." The grace and life of Christ's death and resurrection become available in a most intimate manner for those who worthily participate and receive the very Body and Blood of Christ. Christ feeds us—gives us sustenance that is his very self. We partake of the very life of God in the Eucharist.

The Essentials

Bread made from wheat flour and water, and wine made from grapes, are required for the Eucharist. The intention of the Church is to do as Christ did at the Last Supper. So the same elements are required: not only bread and wine, but the same words as well.

For this reason, the priest at each Mass repeats the words of Jesus over the bread and wine. An ordained priest is also required for the consecration of the bread and wine. The priest, who stands in the place of Christ, the one High Priest, must be a man. Again, the Church follows the direction of Christ to his disciples—direction that has been handed on through the Tradition of the Church for twenty centuries.

In the words of the consecration at each Mass, the bread and wine become the Body and Blood, the very Soul and Divinity, of Christ—a process that is formally referred to as transubstantiation. No meal is complete until the food is eaten. In Communion, the priest and the faithful in attendance receive Christ under the appearances of the bread and wine.

The Unfolding of the Drama

The awesomeness of the essence of Eucharist is surrounded by words, actions, and symbols that augment the basic reality. Catholic Mass is divided into two general parts: the Liturgy of the Word and the Liturgy of the Eucharist.

Because the faithful are coming into God's presence, the Liturgy of the Word begins with a personal consideration of sins by the individual. Then there is a series of scriptural readings, responses, and prayers—an interaction in which God speaks and the faithful give appropriate response.

The Liturgy of the Eucharist begins with the Offertory. The faithful present the bread and wine to the priest—the bread and wine that will become the Body and Blood of Christ. It is a practical gift, since these elements are required for the Eucharist. It is also a symbolic gift, for those in attendance can offer themselves to be transformed along with the bread and wine. Our gifts, trials, hopes, even our failures can be offered along with these simple elements of bread and wine to a God who brings life and meaning.

After the gifts are brought to the altar, the priest will mix a few drops of water with the wine. There is dual symbolism in this action. First, it is a reminder that in death, blood and water flowed from the side of Jesus. The water also represents the congregation's intentions. Symbolically, we are reminded that our intentions are joined with Christ and will be offered to the Father.

The Eucharistic Prayer follows. A number of approved versions of this prayer are used; all of them have their roots in the ancient prayer of the Church and remind us that this action joins us not only with Christ, but also with Christians throughout history. Despite the variety of Eucharistic prayers, the words of consecration, an essential element of the sacrament, remain the same.

During the words of consecration the congregation usually kneels. This is an acknowledgement of the mystery that is unfolding before them. It is also an appropriate posture before Christ the King, who has become present on the altar.

After the Eucharistic prayer, the priest invites the congregation to pray together the prayer that Jesus taught his disciples. Each individual has offered him or herself with Christ and will individually receive him in Communion. However, as the congregation joins in the prayer of the Our Father, they are reminded that they stand together as a community of faith.

This union is emphasized as the minister invites all present to exchange a sign of peace. Jesus was adamant when he said, "So if you are offering your gift at the altar, and there remember that your brother has something against you, leave your gift there before the altar and go;

first be reconciled to your brother, and then come and offer your gift" (Mt 5:23-24). This sign of peace provides the opportunity for such reconciliation to take place in our hearts.

The individual reception of Jesus is fast approaching at this point of the Mass, so again there is a pause to ask God's forgiveness for sins. The priest raises the Host that has become Christ so that all can see our Lord. He proclaims the truth that resounds through the ages and echoes in heaven: "This is the Lamb of God who takes away the sins of the world. Happy are those called to his supper." The congregation, echoing the words of the Roman centurion in the New Testament (see Mt 8:5-13), responds: "Lord, I am not worthy to receive you, but only say the word and I shall be healed."

No one is worthy to receive the eternal Son of God, but all are in need of this spiritual food. And so Christ offers himself to those in attendance. Communicants approach the minister to receive Christ, truly present under the appearances of bread and wine.

The Church recommends that prior to receiving Communion a simple bow be made by each communicant as an acknowledgement that Christ is present. The priest proclaims the profound reality as he extends the Host and states: "The body of Christ." The communicant responds with an "Amen" as a response of agreement.

Words and Their Meanings

Eucharist is not a word in our ordinary vocabulary. It comes from a Greek word that means "to give thanks." Rather than trying to give some description to the mystery, the name of this sacrament focuses on the appropriate response. The sacrifice of Christ is represented on the altar; grace and life are made available to the faithful. A reality that supersedes all reality can only perhaps be spoken of as Eucharist—thanks to God!

Communion is the word that describes the individual reception of

Christ at Mass. This term evokes the notion of sharing. In this Communion, the recipient shares intimately in the life of the Savior.

Some Rules and Regulations

To emphasize the sacred character of the celebration of Eucharist, the Church has established and maintained certain rules for the reception of Communion. For example, only Catholics may receive the sacrament. The Catholic understanding of Eucharist is unique, and its reception implies both an agreement with that understanding and a unity with the Church.

Those who receive should also be in the state of grace. They should be free from serious (often called "mortal") sin. This matter will be discussed further in the next section. But we should note here that this requirement for receiving Communion is reflected in the Scripture, which states: "Whoever ... eats the bread or drinks the cup of the Lord in an unworthy manner will be guilty of profaning the body and blood of the Lord" (1 Cor 11:27).

The Church also requires Catholics to attend the Eucharistic celebration each Sunday, unless there is a serious reason that would prohibit attendance (such as sickness or the unavailability of a priest). This is only reasonable since, as we have noted, the Eucharist is the source and summit of the Christian life. Christians need the spiritual food and graces that are offered at the Mass. Men and women by their very nature need to worship God. Considering the great benefit of the Mass, the Church's expectation that we would attend it weekly seems to be the merest of requirements.

In addition, the Church has always urged the faithful to fast prior to receiving our Lord in the Eucharist. This is a tradition of long standing, but the length of the fast has varied over the years. At present the communicant is to fast from food and drink (other than water) for at least one hour before reception of Communion. This act of reverence is to help dispose the body, heart, and mind to the unique Gift that is to be received.

Personal and Family Customs

Many individuals and families add personal devotions and customs to their celebration of the Eucharist. For example, some will avoid television and radio prior to Mass to allow the opportunity to focus on the Lord Jesus. Some families will share a special breakfast after Mass and perhaps invite others to join with them. This emphasizes the communal aspect of Eucharist and the nature of celebration that is inherent in it.

Some family traditions have been handed on for generations and continue to serve as a call to reverence and celebration.

Staying the Course—the Sacrament of Reconciliation

At times illness leaves us weak, unable to work or function normally in life. Some sickness is even life-threatening. At these times we see a doctor, submit our symptoms to his or her scrutiny and then, willingly, take the medicine that is prescribed. The process may not be enjoyable, but the outcome is welcomed: We are restored to health.

Sin weakens us in our spiritual life. It saps our spiritual strength and makes us less effective as disciples of Christ. If the sin is serious and is neglected, it can be life-threatening—eternal-life-threatening. So Christ instituted a sacrament to help us with spiritual sickness. It is called the sacrament of Penance and Reconciliation or, more popularly, Confession.

Similar to physical recovery from illness, spiritual recovery from sin through the sacrament of Reconciliation involves a process. The penitent confesses his or her sin to an ordained priest, just as patients tell their symptoms to the doctor. The priest, as an instrument of Christ, will grant absolution and assign a penance—parallel to the therapy or medicine that the doctor may prescribe.

Origin

Christ instituted this sacrament when he told his disciples: "Receive the Holy Spirit. If you forgive the sins of any, they are forgiven; if you retain the sins of any, they are retained" (Jn 20:22-23). The practice of this sacrament can be traced back to the early Church. However, there has been significant development since that time in the understanding of the sacrament.

In the Roman Empire the Church made many converts, so Baptism was often administered to adults. Baptism grants remission of sins. The sacrament of Penance was available but was used primarily for the forgiveness of *serious* sins that were committed after Baptism. The penances assigned were often severe and public; a penitent could be required, for example, to make a major pilgrimage or to sit outside the church in rags for a specific period of time. The weight of the penance imposed reflected the serious nature of the sin.

In time other aspects of the sacrament received greater attention. Not only was it a means to receive forgiveness for serious sin; Christians came to realize that the grace of the sacrament strengthened the individual to maintain a strong Christian life and avoid serious sin. To return to the previous parallel with physical illness, going to Confession was like taking vitamins to deal with minor deficiencies and to stay healthy.

The Essentials

The sacrament of Reconciliation normally requires the involvement of three individuals. First, there must be a penitent who has sins, either mortal or venial, to confess. The second person is Christ, for it is he who forgives sins and imparts grace. The trio is completed with the priest, who by the power of his office acts as the agent of Christ in the sacrament.

Why is it necessary to have a priest? The reasons are many. The primary reason is that Christ gave the authority to forgive sins to his apostles as part of their priestly ministry. Yet there are other important reasons as well.

Every sin is an offense against both Christ and his Church. Therefore, the involvement not only of Christ but also of another member of the Church is appropriate. An additional advantage to confession to a priest is the objectivity that he brings to the process. The "guesswork" of forgiveness is removed. "If we confess our sins, he [Christ] is faithful and just, and will forgive our sins and cleanse us from all unrighteousness" (1 Jn 1:9).

The priest, speaking for Christ, gives the words of absolution: "I absolve you from your sins in the name of the Father, and of the Son, and of the Holy Spirit." The power that Christ gave to his apostles is effective. The penitent who comes with right intention receives forgiveness of his or her sin. Grace is imparted to strengthen the forgiven to avoid sin and live a Christian life.

In the Box

The sacrament of Reconciliation can be celebrated[6] at any time or at any place. Traditionally a "box" or room called a *confessional* is utilized. For many years the common practice for the penitent was to kneel behind a screen with the priest seated on the other side. This method is still the option chosen by many.

The penitent seeks forgiveness from Christ through the priest. Christ knows the penitent. However, it is not important for the agent, the priest, to know the individual. For some it can be helpful in freely confessing personal sin to be removed from face-to-face contact. In addition, since the priest is to dispense the sacrament based on the sincere contrition of the penitent, a degree of anonymity removes the influences of any personal prejudice.

Since Vatican II, however, the practice of face-to-face confession has evolved. In this approach the emphasis is upon forgiveness and reconciliation rather than on the confession of sins. The priest can pray with the individual and offer counsel in ways that were formerly encumbered by "secret" confession.

In the end the Church leaves the decision to the individual penitent and priest.

"I'm Sorry" Is Not Enough

The effectiveness of Confession as a sacrament is dependent not only upon the grace of God, but also upon the attitude and actions of the one seeking forgiveness and reconciliation with God. The first requirement for a worthy reception of the sacrament is *contrition*. This means more than merely an emotional "feeling sorry."

Contrition must be more than outward show. It must be true and arise from the heart, the soul, the decision of the mind. This does not mean that the penitent needs "perfect contrition," which involves a sorrow motivated purely by love of God. An imperfect sorrow, in which one is contrite because of fear of eternal punishment, can be sufficient for the sacrament.

In either case, contrition also requires that the penitent wants to change and is willing to respond to grace and make a sincere effort to avoid sin in the future.

Speak It

The next requirement of the penitent is that he or she must actually verbally confess particular sins. It is not enough to say: "I have sinned." The penitent needs to name a specific sin: "I lied" or "I stole a television." This self-accusation should be made truthfully and humbly. In addition, confession must be made in person. You can't phone in or e-mail your confession!

Penance

The priest will assign a *penance* for the individual. This may include saying certain prayers, reading certain texts for reflection, or taking some particular action—for example, restitution of something stolen or some other good act. The Church has always taught that sin is forgiven by the free gift of Christ alone. The penitent doesn't gain forgiveness by saying ten Hail Marys. Nevertheless, the Church also teaches that there is temporal punishment for sin—our actions have consequences.

If I strike my friend and then ask forgiveness, he may forgive me, but he will probably still have a bruise from the blow. Penance deals not with forgiveness for the blow, but rather with the bruise that is caused. Often the priest will match the penance to the sin. For the sacrament to be complete, the penitent must perform the assigned penance.

The Seal of Confession

There is no need to worry that what you confess to a priest will become street corner gossip. The priest is bound to keep secret what he has heard in Confession. This maintenance of secrecy and privacy in the sacrament is called "the seal." The priest may not speak about the matter of Confession to anyone outside of the confessional—even the one who confessed the sin.

Count It All Joy

The sacrament of Reconciliation is a great blessing to Catholics. To hear those words uttered by the priest, "Your sin is forgiven," brings great freedom. A burden is lifted. A wound is healed. A fresh start is undertaken. Thus frequent Confession is recommended to Catholics because of the grace it brings to help them live as disciples of Christ.

Again, to draw on our previous medical analogy, we can note that regular checkups are the best means to stay healthy. In a similar way, regular, sincere Confession keeps a Catholic spiritually healthy.

A Life Together—Marriage

In 1951 the famous Archishop Fulton Sheen wrote a book entitled *Three to Get Married.* The book is still in publication today. The title sounds almost scandalous—three partners in a marriage? However, that reality is exactly the basis for the sacrament of Matrimony. The Catholic marriage has three parties: the man, the woman, and God.

The definition and formalization of the sacrament of Matrimony actually came late in the history of the Church. It wasn't until about the year 1000 that the sacramental definition of marriage was fully developed. However, this does not mean that Christian marriage was not considered a sacrament prior to that date. Christ elevated marriage to a higher level by pointing to God's original intent in the union of a man and a woman: "From the beginning of creation, 'God made them male and female.' For this reason a man shall leave his father and mother and be joined to his wife, and the two shall become one.... What therefore God has joined together, let not man put asunder" (Mk 10:6-9). Many other passages in the New Testament also witness to the sacred nature of marriage (see, for example, 1 Cor 7 and Eph 5).

Early Church fathers such as St. Augustine and St. Ambrose wrote about the sacramental nature of marriage. But marriage is not only a sacrament; it is also a "natural" union. Therefore, it took time to define the sacramental nature of this union.

What's the Matter?

In discussing the other sacraments, we've focused on the essentials of the sacrament—those elements that must be present to make the sacrament valid. Usually there is a tangible element, such as water in Baptism. This is called the *matter*.

There also are prescribed words and actions. Baptism requires the pouring of water while saying the formula: "I baptize you in the name of the Father ..." This activity is called the *form*.

Finally, there is a minister of the sacrament. Most often this person is a bishop, priest, or deacon, although it can on occasion be a layperson. (For example, anyone can baptize in an emergency situation.)

Most Catholics can make a good guess as to the matter, form, and minister of most sacraments. The notable exception is usually the sacrament of Matrimony. So what is the matter of this sacrament? The man and woman themselves are the matter of the sacrament. They are also the ministers of the sacrament. It is their consent, which will later be consummated by sexual intercourse, that comprises the form.

The obvious question, then, is how does a sacramental marriage differ from a purely natural marriage? First, the couple to be joined must be baptized—a sacramental marriage is not possible between two unbaptized individuals. Baptism has brought these two individuals into God's family. As they make their mutual free consent before God, he, their heavenly Father, bestows his blessing and grace.

Normally the marriage will take place within the context of a Mass, and a priest or deacon will preside. This setting affirms the sacramental nature of the union and brings the blessing not only of God but also of the assembled body of believers and of the entire Church.

Consent

The exchange of *consent* is the key element in the marriage ceremony. Popularly this consent is called the "exchange of vows." Although this is not a formal title, it does signify the basis of the consent, because a vow is a "free and deliberate promise." In the case of marriage, this promise is made to the partner before God and in the presence of the community.

The marriage bond is a *covenant* relationship. A covenant implies a deeper bond than a mere contract. Contracts are usually made binding by some promise of a material item. ("If I don't fulfill my promise, I'll pay you so much money") However, a covenant is a "life" promise: It binds two lives together. In essence, the parties of a covenant are willing to lay down their lives for the other party.

Jesus is referred to as the author of the New Covenant. He laid down his life on the cross for the Church. Marriage, as a covenant relationship, is a sign of this covenant between Christ and the Church.

One particular formula is customary to express consent in wedding services: "I take you to be my husband...." However, the formula can vary.[7]

Rings

In many Western cultures the couple exchanges rings as a sign of their consent and commitment. Although a profound sign, this action is not a requirement of the ritual. For the majority who wish to exchange rings, a blessing is included within the marriage rite for the ring ceremony.

Witnesses

Almost every wedding has a best man and a maid of honor. These guests fulfill the requirement of the Church's canon law that at least two witnesses be present at the marriage ceremony. Normally a priest or deacon will also assist at the marriage.

As a sacrament, marriage is a celebration of the entire community. The presence of the community emphasizes the unity of the faithful in the body of Christ. To celebrate the marriage ceremony within the context of a Mass emphasizes the relationship between the sacrament of marriage and the sacrament of the Eucharist.

Norms

The Church has put in place several norms concerning marriage. For example, because marriage is a lifelong commitment, the Church requires couples to undergo some preparation before the marriage ceremony. The type of preparation, however, may vary significantly from diocese to diocese.

The marriage normally takes place in the parish of either the bride or the groom. Marriage within the context of a Mass can be celebrated on any day of the week. (Sundays require the bishop's permission.) But couples often avoid scheduling their wedding Mass during Advent and Lent because of the penitential nature of these seasons.

Customs

Many ethnic and cultural celebrations are associated with marriage. In the Mexican culture, for example, a rope or cincture is placed over the shoulders of the couple after the gospel of the Mass. This is to signify the binding tie of the marriage.

A long-standing tradition for many couples is the placement of flowers before a statue of the Blessed Mother after the wedding ceremony. This custom both honors Mary and asks her intercession.

Many families also have a brief ceremony prior to the wedding when the parents of the bride and groom impart a special blessing on the couple.

Differences in the East

In the Eastern Church, the priest is a more integral part of the sacrament. There, the blessing of the priest is required for the validity of the sacrament. In addition, in most Eastern Churches the wedding service is divided into two parts. The first part consists of the consent between the couple. The second part, the Crowning, includes a blessing administered by the priest or bishop.

More Than a Day

Marriage is a sacrament that is meant to have an ongoing and lasting impact on the couple. The grace of the sacrament is available to help the couple throughout their marriage. For that reason, the annual wedding anniversary can be more than a remembering of a past event.

Many couples take the opportunity on their anniversary to renew their commitment to each other. Praying together daily as a couple is another wonderful practice to remain open to God's guidance and strengthening.

Divorce and Annulment

A true sacramental marriage is a lifelong relationship that serves as a sign of the relationship between Christ and the Church. Two individuals have become one in a bond that cannot be broken. Therefore, in accordance with the teaching of Christ and the Tradition of the Church, a true sacramental marriage cannot be broken.

On occasion, a civil divorce may be obtained by one of the marriage partners for serious legal or safety issues. However, this action does not break the true marriage bond, and the parties are not free to remarry.

For a valid marriage to take place, the essential elements of the marriage must be present and "the consent must be an act of the will of each of the contracting parties."[8] The key concept is that the consent must be "free" and that the individuals are capable of making the consent. Someone cannot be coerced into marriage, then, and the person must be psychologically able to give a free consent.

If this freedom is lacking, or if any of a number of other essential aspects of marriage are lacking, there is no marriage. In such a case, the couple can ask the Church to review the situation and make a declaration as to whether a true marriage exists. If the Church finds that one or both parties did not make a true and free consent, the Church will declare the marriage null. This process is called an *annulment.*

An annulment is not a divorce. A divorce would be the breaking of a valid marriage bond, while an annulment is the recognition that a marriage never existed between the two individuals.

Holy Orders

We all have a vocation—that is, a calling from God to a particular state in life. Most people are called to marriage. Others are called to live in the single state, some as religious sisters or brothers. The third possibility is the ordained priesthood. The sacrament for the ordination to the ranks of deacon, priest, or bishop is called Holy Orders.

Jesus chose apostles and commissioned them to carry on the sacramental aspects of his ministry. In reality, Jesus is the ultimate priest. He is the minister and primary mediator of all grace. Men who are ordained priests "act in the power and place of the person of Christ,"[9] becoming delegates and channels of Christ when they function in their ministry.

The ordained ministry has three degrees. Bishops have the fullness of Holy Orders. They are the successors of the apostles. An unbroken chain of bishops stretches through history from the time of the apostles to the present; this chain is called the *apostolic succession.*

The apostles ordained men to carry on the priestly ministry as bishops. These successors then passed the authority to other men, and so on up to the present day. Priests have a subordinated degree of Holy Orders and function as co-workers with the bishop in his pastoral and sacramental work.

A deacon—the term means "one who serves"—is the lowest degree of Holy Orders. Some functions, such as the ability to ordain priests and deacons, are reserved to bishops. A priest may hear confession and celebrate the Mass, but a deacon cannot engage in these functions.

Nevertheless, deacons perform many important roles. They assist the bishop and priests in the celebration of the Eucharist. They have the authority to proclaim the Gospel and to preach at Mass, to distribute Communion, to assist at and bless marriages, and to preside at funerals. In addition, they give themselves to various ministries of charity and pastoral government.

Essentials

Only a bishop can administer the sacrament of Holy Orders, for he alone, as successor to the apostles, has the fullness of authority to do so. A bishop may only be ordained by a papal decree or papal approbation.

The ordination of a priest is administered at a Mass normally celebrated at the Cathedral Church. The sacrament is administered when the bishop lays his hands upon the head of the candidate and prays the prayer of consecration.

Men Only

Only baptized men can be admitted in the sacrament of Orders. This provision has been affirmed as an essential part of the sacrament.

It is true that the close followers of Jesus included women. Women have been key in the work and ministry of the Church from the time of Jesus until today. However, when Jesus set up the ordained priesthood, he specifically chose twelve men.

The Church is entrusted with passing on the faith that has been received from Christ. Therefore, it is not within the power of the Church to change the practice of ordaining only men. In fact, it is apparent that throughout the history of the Catholic Church only men have been ordained.

In 1994 Pope John Paul II reiterated this teaching: "I declare that the Church has no authority whatsoever to confer priestly ordination on women and that this judgment is to be definitively held by all the Church's faithful."

Women play an active role in the Church as laywomen and as consecrated single women, such as nuns. Nevertheless, only males can be ordained.

Celibacy

Celibacy is "the discipline of the Latin Church that forbids ordained ministers to marry."[10] This definition provides some important information.

First, celibacy is a *discipline*. A discipline is a rule imposed by the Church to foster the life and health of the Church. Abstaining from eating meat on Fridays is a discipline of the Church that has been relaxed in recent times. In a similar way, celibacy could be changed. However, we should note that this discipline has a long-standing tradition in the Church and has proved to be of great value.

Priestly celibacy is particular to the Western (Latin) Church. In the Eastern Catholic Church, a married man can be ordained a priest. However, if his wife should die, he could not remarry, and only celibate men can be chosen to serve as bishops in the Eastern Catholic Churches.

In both the Eastern and Western Churches, permanent deacons[11] may be married at the time of ordination.

The tradition of a celibate priesthood has its roots in the New Testament and has been a firmly established tradition since the early Middle Ages. As with the theological training required for priests, the Church requires celibacy not because God commands it, but rather because it is a valuable practice.

Perspective

Some people blame a celibate male priesthood for various problems and difficulties in the Catholic Church. However, it is important to keep a proper perspective on this characteristic of Catholic clergy.

First, ordination does not make a man a saint. Holy Orders does grant sacramental powers to the recipient and does give graces for the fulfillment of the office of deacon, priest, or bishop. Yet these men are still subject to temptation and sin that plagues all men and women. Their lives, like the lives of married couples, are a lifelong struggle to cooperate with God's grace and remain faithful. That some will fail or fall short of the lofty goal to which they are called is to be expected.

Even so, the priesthood is a wonderful provision that Christ gave the Church. The value of the priesthood has been ratified throughout the Church's history. Perhaps we should be amazed at how many priests have led lives of outstanding virtue and courage. Any study of the list of canonized saints will verify that the Church has been blessed by many godly priests.

Healing and Grace for Death and New Life

"Is any among you sick? Let him call for the elders of the church, and let them pray over him, anointing him with oil in the name of the Lord; and the prayer of faith will save the sick man, and the Lord will raise him up, and if he has committed sins, he will be forgiven" (Jas 5:14-15). These words from the New Testament are one of the key scriptural references to the sacrament known as the Anointing of the Sick.

The practice of this sacrament can be traced to some of the earliest writings of the Church fathers. However, it has undergone a variety of changes over the centuries. From earliest times the sacrament was known as the "Anointing of the Sick" or the "Office of Anointing." But around the twelfth century the understanding and use of the sacrament narrowed. Especially in the Western Church, the focus of the sacrament became "the dying" rather than merely "the sick." The common name for this anointing became "Extreme Unction" and was reserved for those in "grave … danger of death."[12]

Since Vatican Council II, however, the Church has rediscovered the earlier, broader understanding of the sacrament. Once again it is known as the "Anointing of the Sick." The focus is once more on those who are "tried by illness."[13]

As Pope Paul VI explains, the Anointing of the Sick "is not a sacrament for those only who are at the point of death. Hence, as soon as any one of the faithful begins to be in danger of death from sickness or old age, the fitting time for them to receive this sacrament has already arrived."[14]

In the past this sacrament was administered to the individual on his or her deathbed. Nevertheless, as with all sacraments, anointing has a communal aspect. Thus the revised rite encourages the participation of the faithful.

This participation may mean that the family members take a more active role if the sacrament is administered in a hospital or home. There now are also communal celebrations of the sacrament especially for the elderly. Often these communal celebrations take place within the context of the Eucharist.

The Essentials

The recipient for this sacrament must be a baptized Christian with a "serious" sickness or the effects of old age. The appropriate minister is a priest. The priest lays his hands upon the sick person, anoints him or her with oil, and prays the prayer as specified in the liturgical text for this sacrament.

Some of the liturgical prayers are offered for physical healing. Nevertheless, a key focus of the prayers is the request for grace to comfort and strengthen the afflicted person spiritually, along with a petition that God would forgive the individual's sins.

The oil used in this sacrament has normally been blessed by the bishop. It signifies a strengthening and the presence of the Holy Spirit.

Often the Anointing of the Sick is preceded by the sacrament of Reconciliation and followed by the Eucharist. Thus the person struggling with the illness receives the grace of three sacraments.

Grab the Grace

"Should we call the priest?" is a question often asked by family members when someone is ill. Some Catholics are reluctant to make that call because they don't want to upset the sick person with thoughts of the possibility of death. Nevertheless, probably no greater gift can be given to a seriously ill person than the grace of the sacrament of Anointing.

Christian Death and Burial

Death for the Catholic involves a degree of celebration, because death is actually another birth. For the faithful, death ends life on earth, but it also brings the transition to eternal life with God. Although no sacrament is associated exclusively with death, there are prayers, ceremonies, and traditions to accompany the deceased on their passage while also offering hope and consolation to the living.

When a Catholic dies, the community offers prayers for him or her. Death may cause physical separation, but not separation in faith. All the baptized are members of the body of Christ, and Christ has only one body. So whether someone is on this side of the grave or on the other side, a relationship remains because of membership in the same body. Just as prayers can be offered for a living neighbor who can be seen, so too prayers can be offered for a deceased neighbor who no longer can be seen.

When people die, their fate is sealed. Human destiny lies either in heaven or hell. However, for those bound for heaven there can be a process of purification. Traditionally, this process is called *purgatory*.

Belief in purgatory is the admission that although someone is saved through Jesus, he or she may not be ready to stand before a perfect God. Prayers that God's grace would be active on behalf of the deceased can be offered for those in that process of purification.

Love can reach beyond the grave. So the Church makes available various liturgical prayers for the deceased. "The Order of Christian Funerals" contains prayers to be used immediately after death, in the vigil at the funeral home, in a funeral Mass, and at the place of burial.

The Church strongly recommends a funeral Mass as the central event in the funeral process. As the Eucharist sustained the believer in life, so in death, the Mass can be offered for the deceased.

The Cemetery

Only three major religious traditions have made the cemetery a significant element in their faith: the Jewish, Catholic, and Orthodox traditions. The Catholic Church has maintained cemeteries because of our belief that even in death the body should be treated with respect. Most Catholic cemeteries have provisions for the burial of the poor so that all Catholics have an opportunity to be buried in a Catholic cemetery, if one is available.

A cemetery is identified as "Catholic" if it has been specifically blessed by the local bishop or his designee for the burial of Catholics and their families. Burial in a Catholic cemetery continues the sense of community that is apparent in the parish and diocesan structure.

The faithful are not obliged to be buried in a Catholic cemetery.

When burial occurs in a cemetery that is not Catholic, the priest (or other presider at the committal) blesses the specific grave or crypt where the burial will occur.

There was a time when Catholics were not permitted to be cremated. This practice was not allowed because some religious traditions cremate their deceased as a sign that they reject the Catholic belief in the resurrection of the dead.[15] Today, however, cremation may be chosen for economic or space reasons. Thus Catholics may now be cremated and granted the full liturgical rites of the Church. Nonetheless, it is recommended that the funeral Mass be celebrated in the presence of the full body and that cremation occur after the funeral Mass.

Family Involvement

The Catholic funeral rite provides many opportunities for the involvement of the family in the rite and prayers. This involvement allows the surviving family to participate in final acts of love for the deceased person.

In all these ways, then, we see how the seven sacraments of the Catholic Church, and the traditions that surround them, provide ways to express the love relationship between God and his people. From womb to tomb, Christ and his Church stand ready with sacramental graces to offer blessings, strength, and hope for those who ask.

TWO

Times and Seasons

To everything, turn, turn, turn,
there is a season, turn, turn,
and a time for every purpose under heaven.

These lyrics from a popular song of the 1960s reappeared in a successful movie of the 1990s. But these words in their original form come from the Bible (see Eccl 3:1-9). They reflect the Catholic belief that all times and seasons are in God's hands, and that God has a purpose.

History has a direction. There is an end, a goal to be reached. The goal is an ever-closer union with God that will culminate in eternal life with him in heaven. For that reason, the Church year is divided into times and seasons meant to help Catholics in the journey of life toward that goal.

Liturgical seasons and feasts are more than memorials to past events. They also allow Catholics to enter into the mystery of Christ's redemptive life, death, and resurrection and to join in the lives of the saints that have preceded us. Thus they become opportunities for grace and growth.

The times and seasons celebrated in the Church's liturgical year are full of the stuff of human life: sorrow, joy, failure, repentance, renewal, hope. So each of us can identify and visualize our personal life as part of this yearly drama.

But these times and seasons are also the stuff of divine life. They can help us break the bounds of mortal life and communicate with God. Those who seriously enter into these times and seasons can be transformed by the life (Jesus himself) they encounter there. God works through the Church's liturgy to provide grace, strength, and direction to those who wish to draw closer to him.

This divine help is communicated in and through tangible realities. Things we can feel, see, smell, and touch combine with the decisions of the human will to provide an avenue where divine life is available.

Each of us lives though the same annual cycle of the seasons of spring, summer, winter, and fall. There is something comforting in the yearly flow of these seasons. Yet we all know that each year we experience something new in the context of those familiar times and seasons.

So, too, the liturgical calendar provides a familiarity that grounds us in the life of the Church. This road of the Church year can be traveled each year without ever growing wearisome or old because, in Christ, life is always new.

Advent

Imagine the level of excitement in your home if you just learned that the president of the United States was coming for dinner in four weeks. You would want to shine the silver service, get out the best dishes, mow the lawn, and have your best suit cleaned. You would be enthusiastic in telling all your friends and family about the important guest. Preparing for that guest would change your life.

The term *advent* is based on a Latin word that describes the coming or visitation of the emperor. It is an ideal word to describe the first season of the Catholic Church's liturgical year. This is the season that anticipates the coming of Christ the King. Just as if we were waiting for the president to arrive for dinner, we have much to accomplish before the anticipated day.

In a sense, the season of Advent actually celebrates and anticipates three comings of Christ. First is the historic coming of Christ that occurred about two thousand years ago. Advent recalls the long period of waiting and preparation of the Hebrew people before the arrival of Jesus on that first Christmas day.

Reviewing this history gives Catholics an appreciation of the significance of the Incarnation (when God took on human nature and was born of Mary). To celebrate the birth of any individual is appropriate. To celebrate the birth of the God-Man who came to save all humankind is vital. The preparation for this celebration is a key focus of Advent.

Yet Jesus did not live only for thirty-three years and then disappear from the lives of his people. The fact is that he still lives in the hearts and spirits of all baptized Christians. Therefore the preparation and anticipation of Advent is an opportunity to deepen the life of Christ in the individual. Catholics long to have the life of Christ renewed in their lives—just as the ancient Hebrews longed for the Messiah to come to them.

Two key figures appear in the readings of the Advent season. One is John the Baptist, the precursor of Christ. He proclaimed repentance to the Jews, encouraging them to prepare for the coming of the Messiah. John expressed a sentiment that should be a guiding principle for every Catholic: "He [Jesus] must increase, but I must decrease" (Jn 3:30).

The other Advent figure is Mary. When the angel Gabriel appeared to Mary and announced that she was to be the Mother of the Savior, she responded: "Let it be to me according to your word" (Lk 1:38). She accepted the Son of God into her life.

Mary's life was typified by obedience to the will of God and a spirit that was docile to God, joined to a firmness in her willingness to endure hardship. These are character traits in which every Catholic can find inspiration.

Mary and John the Baptist are our models and guides during Advent. Heeding the call of John the Baptist, we want to examine our lives, repent where needed, and set things right in our hearts so that Jesus can find a home there. In essence, this is a second kind of "coming" of Christ that we celebrate in Advent. Like Mary, we are encouraged to say yes to God—to allow him to live in a more intimate way in our lives.

Yet another coming of Christ is celebrated in Advent. Jesus was born in Bethlehem two thousand years ago. He remains with us as the head of his mystical body, the Church, and in the heart of every Christian. Nevertheless, as the creed proclaims, Jesus will also come again in glory at the end of time.

This coming will be the culmination of the redemptive plan of God. The final judgment and the establishment of "a new heaven and a new earth" will take place, when all will acknowledge the glory and power of God. Then all of the saved will dwell for eternity in true bliss with God.

Christians long for this fulfillment of the plan and promise of God. So Advent is a time to prepare, anticipate, and pray for that last coming of Jesus when "God will wipe away every tear" (Rv 7:17).

History

The Church's universal celebration of the birth of Christ dates from the fifth century. Only a short time later, the Church set aside a season prior to Christmas as preparation for that feast. In many parts of the Christian world, the faithful were encouraged to fast or practice other signs of penance to prepare for Christmas. In some local churches the time period of preparation was only a few days, while in other churches the length of preparation was as much as five weeks. Eventually the period of the four Sundays prior to Christmas and the accompanying weekdays were set as the time of Advent for the Western Church.

Liturgy

How many mothers have said to their children: "If you want Santa to bring you presents, you had better be good!" The children are then filled with anticipation and wonder as they strive to be on their best behavior.

The Church presents a similar mix of themes in the season of Advent. The tone of the liturgies and the selection of the readings are filled with the theme of anticipation—Jesus is coming! On the third Sunday of Advent the priest often wears a rose-colored vestment to emphasize the joy of anticipating the coming of Christ.

Yet there is also a more somber mood. We need to be prepared to meet Jesus, who, while full of mercy, is also just. So the Church encourages a degree of penance and mortification in Advent to prepare the mind and spirit for a deeper, more intimate relationship with Jesus.

During the initial Sundays of Advent, the call of John the Baptist is heard: "Repent, for the kingdom of heaven is at hand" (Mt 3:2). Accordingly, for three of the weeks of Advent the priest wears violet vestments, a sign of repentance. As another sign of penance, the exuberant *Gloria* is omitted during the Sunday Mass. It is not heard again until the Christmas Vigil Mass, just as the shepherds heard it sung by angels on that first Christmas Eve.

Advent Wreath

A number of traditions are connected with the Advent season. Many of these traditions, while outside of the official liturgy of the Church, enhance the celebration of the season. One of the most popular symbols of this time of preparation is the Advent wreath.

The traditional Advent wreath is a circle of evergreen branches into which are placed four candles: three colored violet, and one, rose. The first Sunday one candle is lit; each Sunday after, an additional candle is lit. The progressive lighting heightens the sense of anticipation of the coming of Jesus.

Evergreen is a symbol of continuous life. The circular configuration points to the eternity of God, who has no beginning and no end. The flame is a reminder that we await Jesus, who is the Light of the world. The three violet candles correspond to the liturgical vestments of Advent and emphasize the need for repentance and good works to prepare for Christ's arrival. The rose candle is lit on the third Sunday, which is known as *Gaudete* ("Rejoice!") Sunday, a time to rejoice at the fact that the awaited arrival is near.

Jesse Tree

Many people enjoy exploring their heritage. It not only helps them understand from where they came, but also gives them a perspective on their present life. That, in part, is the purpose of the Jesse tree.

In many ways the Old Testament shows the "roots" of the coming of Jesus. Catholics are people of the New Testament who have their spiritual heritage in the Old Testament. The Old Testament is the unfolding story of preparation for the coming of the promised Messiah, a story that culminates in the coming of Jesus. Knowledge of that story and legacy can help Christians gain perspective on the impact of Jesus in their own lives.

The Jesse tree traces salvation history as worked out through the Old Testament. It may be a real tree, usually an evergreen, or it may be a symbolic tree. In either case, the tree brings to mind the words from Isaiah 11:1: "There shall come forth a shoot from the stump of Jesse, and a branch shall grow out of his roots." Jesse was the father of David, the greatest king of Israel. David was an ancestor and prefiguring of Jesus, the ultimate king of Israel and of the world.

On each day of Advent, symbols that represent various biblical characters are placed on this tree. For example, a rainbow symbolizes Noah, a ladder refers to Jacob, and a carpenter's square recalls Joseph, the foster father of Jesus. The symbols are placed on the tree in chronological order starting with Adam. Normally when the symbol is placed on the tree, the story of the individual is told. Each subsequent individual and story moves closer to the culmination, the birth of Jesus.

Other Customs

Because preparation for Christmas so strongly captures the attention of people, both young and old, it is an ideal time to use various customs and traditions to teach the faith and encourage devotion. Some families use the writing of Christmas cards as a time of praying for friends and families. The Catholic bishops of the United States have published blessings that the family can use when setting up the Christmas tree or crèche.

Christmas

Historically, Christmas was not the first feast to be celebrated by the universal Church; Easter holds that place of honor. Only in the early fourth century can historians say with some certainty that Christmas was being celebrated as a part of the liturgical year in Rome. Originally the day was referred to as the birth of Christ or the Nativity. The word *Christmas*, meaning "the Mass of Christ," came into use only in the eleventh century among English speakers.

Nevertheless, today the celebration of Christ's birth is arguably the most popular of Catholic feasts. The Church provides four separate Masses that can be celebrated on Christmas: the Vigil Mass, Mass at midnight, Mass at dawn, and Mass during the day.

The gospel for the Vigil Mass provides the "family record" (see Mt 1:1-17) of Jesus. Essentially, it summarizes all of salvation history from Abraham to Joseph and Mary, the parents of Jesus.

The gospel for the Mass at dawn focuses attention on the shepherds who, while watching their flocks at night, were prompted by the message of angels and went to "see this thing that [had] happened, which the Lord [had] made known" to them (Lk 2:15).

The Mass during Christmas Day takes a different, more theological, view of the Christmas event as it presents the first eighteen verses of the Gospel of John: "In the beginning was the Word...."

The Midnight Mass has long been seen as the key liturgical celebration of Christmas. It is as if Christians can wait no longer for the coming of Christ. The celebration must begin as the clock announces the arrival of the day!

The entire theme of the Mass is one of rejoicing, for—as its entrance antiphon says—"the Savior is born to the world." The Gospel tells the traditional nativity story from the evangelist Luke: "[Mary] gave birth to her first-born son and wrapped him in swaddling cloths, and laid him in a manger, because there was no place for them in the inn" (Lk 2:7). The Gloria, echoing the song of the angels on the first Christmas, is sung for the first time since the beginning of Advent. Decorations and seasonal music help add to the festive celebration.

The Tree and the Crib

The two most recognizable symbols of Christmas are the Christmas tree and the crèche. The crèche specifically refers to the manger in which the Child Jesus was placed on that first Christmas. More generally, it refers to the entire nativity scene: the manger, the Child, Mary, Joseph, animals, and shepherds.

Depictions of the birth of Christ can be found from the fourth century. However, in the thirteenth century St. Francis of Assisi began the popular representation of the nativity that we see today. Francis developed the display at Christmas in 1223 as a reminder to the faithful of the Incarnation.

Nativity scenes are now placed in most Catholic churches on Christmas Eve and maintained until the Feast of the Epiphany, when the "three Magi" or "wise men" are added to the scene. Many Catholic families make a crib a part of the decorations at home as well. The infant Jesus is placed in the crib on Christmas Eve, often accompanied by family prayer or the reading of the Gospel narrative of Christ's birth.

The tradition of the Christmas tree began in Germany and was brought to America by German immigrants. The evergreen tree is a symbol of eternal life—the gift that Jesus offers to humankind. The original tree decorations were cookies and breads hung on the tree. These were reminders that Jesus is the "Bread of Life." This practice also served as a reminder that all should be thankful for their daily bread.

Various blessings can be used when the tree is erected and decorated to emphasis the religious connotations of the tree.

The Gift and a Gift

Can there be a greater gift than God's becoming man so that humanity could be reunited with God? Gratitude for that greatest gift has been the inspiration for other gift giving at Christmas.

A favorite gift-giver whose story is retold in a popular Christmas song is King Wenceslaus. The fable states that the king saw a poor man gathering wood during Christmastime. The good king had his servant gather provisions, which Wenceslaus personally delivered to the poor family. A king bent low to meet the needs of his subjects. The king had learned well from the King of Kings, Jesus, the meaning of love and giving.

Today the meaning behind the giving of gifts can be lost in commercialism. Nevertheless, many charitable organizations now encourage and facilitate the giving of gifts to the poor during the Yuletide season—a practice that recalls the original intent of the custom.

Good Old St. Nick

Various saints are associated with Christmas, including the Holy Innocents, who were martyred by King Herod when he sought to kill the Christ Child. But the saint most often associated with Christmas is St. Nicholas.

Nicholas was a bishop of Myra in Asia Minor during the fourth century. During a persecution of Christians by the Emperor Diocletian, Bishop Nicholas was imprisoned. Since his death, a long tradition of miracles has been attributed to his intercession.

Perhaps the best-remembered aspect of Nicholas' life is his generosity. Legend affirms that he was from a wealthy family, but even as a layman he gave all his possessions to the poor. One legend says that when he heard of a poor family with three unmarried daughters, Nicholas secretly tossed a bag of gold through the window of the home so that the family could provide the necessary dowry for a wedding. The gold reportedly fell into a stocking that was hanging inside from the window sill—the origin, some say, of the Christmas tradition of filling stockings with goodies.

Later, as bishop, Nicholas continued to assist the poor. He visited prisoners and sailors in the port city. He especially took a concern to meet the needs of children. Although the modern Santa Claus character developed from various roots, his relationship to St. Nicholas and the saint's gift-giving is clear.

Keeping Christ in Christmas

A number of Christmas traditions have roots in faith and in the birth of Christ. Gift-giving is only one example of such a custom. Yet not all Christmas traditions have an explicitly spiritual origin, and some with spiritual roots have lost their religious meanings over time.

Some Christmas traditions even have pagan roots. The Christmas tree would be an example here. It started as a pagan custom, but was adapted for Christian usage. Such non-religious traditions have been given a Christian meaning to enhance the Christian celebration.

Celebrating Christmas sometimes results in a struggle for Catholics because the true meaning of the season can be lost amidst all the commercial hype that surrounds the holiday. Perhaps the key to a meaningful season is to rediscover the religious character of Christmas traditions. In addition, Catholics can implement new traditions at home that help to keep a healthy focus on the true significance of Christmas: God became Man as an infant in Bethlehem.

Lent

Imagine a young woman who is not very athletic but who sees value in being involved in athletics. So every fall she trains for cross-country races. She exercises and eats the right diet for a runner. She closely follows the directions of her coach.

Initially, she isn't very good at running. But practice and training help her improve. Each year she begins a new season, and each year she is better than the previous one. By the time she is a high school senior, she qualifies to run in the state championship.

That young woman's experience is similar to that of many dedicated Catholics who engage in a kind of spiritual athletics. Every year the Church provides them the season of Lent as a time of spiritual training through penance and renewal.

In one sense, Lent is the same routine each year: forty days, fasting and abstinence, more time in Church, increased devotion, almsgiving. But there's a good reason why we have to repeat the discipline annually: Catholics are not one-season wonders! St. Paul tells us that we are in a race (see 1 Cor 9:24; 2 Tm 4:7) and we compete for a prize in Christ Jesus (see Phil 3:14). To be a winning athlete takes time, effort, and dedication: "Every athlete exercises self-control in all things. They do it to receive a perishable wreath, but we an imperishable" (1 Cor 9:25).

Lent is an intense period of training. That's not to say that the Catholic isn't striving to "stay in spiritual shape" during the rest of the liturgical year. It is to say that there is value in setting a specific period of time for a more concentrated effort of preparation. Lent is celebrated yearly because we need to keep striving for the "upward call" to be perfect even as Jesus is perfect. Reaching that goal is a lifelong task, but a yearly Lent can move an individual closer to the goal.

Historical Perspective

The Resurrection is the central tenet of the Catholic faith. As Scripture declares: "If Christ has not been raised, then our preaching is in vain and your faith is in vain" (1 Cor 15:14). Each Sunday since biblical times, the Resurrection has been celebrated by the faithful as they gather for the Eucharist. Similarly, each Friday the death of Jesus has been remembered. Thus Sunday has long been a day of celebration, while Friday has been a day of penance and fasting.

Eventually, as the liturgical calendar took shape, an annual celebration of Easter developed. This celebration did not replace the weekly celebration, but augmented it. In conjunction with the yearly celebration of Easter, the Church developed a yearly season of repentance and fasting to prepare for that yearly celebration of the Resurrection.

Moses and the Israelites wandered for forty years in the desert as they prepared to enter the promised land of freedom and life (see Nm 14:33-34). Jesus fasted for forty days prior to beginning his public ministry (see Lk 4:1-14). Thus forty days became the standard for the Christian period of preparation.

Ashes

In both the Old and New Testaments, ashes are associated with mourning and repentance (see, for example, Est 4:1-3; Jb 42:6; Ps 102:9; Mt 11:21.) Thus Lent begins with the celebration of Ash Wednesday. After the reading of the Gospel and the preaching of the homily on this day, the priest blesses ashes with holy water and a prayer. He then invites those in attendance to come forward and receive the imposition of these ashes on their foreheads.

Like a splash of cold water to the face that awakens a person at the beginning of a new day, ashes on the forehead are to awaken the recipient to the beginning of a new season in the Church's liturgical year. These ashes are produced by burning palm branches from the previous year's Palm Sunday celebration; in this way, the year has come full cycle. It is once again time to examine oneself and prepare for a new Easter.

When the ashes are administered the priest or deacon has two formulae of words he can use. "Turn away from sin and be faithful to the Gospel" is the message of Lent. "Remember, man, you are dust, and to dust you will return" impresses the recipient with the fact that now is the time to act—now is the time to get right with God.

Penitential Practices

Lent is the season for turning away from sin and living a life more conformed to the will and plan of God. Penitential practices are a means to that end. Like diet and exercise for the athlete, prayer, mortification, and almsgiving are ways for the Catholic to grow in faith and get closer to Jesus.

A greater focus on prayer may include an effort to attend Mass more often, a trip to a shrine, or a resolve to be more cognizant of God's presence throughout the day. Almsgiving is an exercise of the virtue of charity. It is giving money or goods for the needs of the poor.

The "Lenten rice bowl" has become one popular means of practicing almsgiving by giving up some food at each meal and then setting aside the money that is saved for the needy.

Two prominent means of mortification during Lent are discussed below: fasting and abstinence. However, another form of mortification might be to turn off the television more often and then visit the sick instead, or perhaps read a spiritual book. Mortification can also be walking to the corner store instead of driving and taking the time while walking to say a decade of the rosary.

The advantages of penitential practices are many. First, they remind us that we are sinners in need of Christ's salvation. They also make a statement that we are serious about overcoming the sin in our lives.

These practices can dispose us to hear God more clearly and to receive his grace. They do not win us salvation nor do they garner "points" toward heaven. Salvation and eternal life are gifts of God to those who believe and walk in his ways. Acts of mortification, when undertaken in a spirit of penance, help us to grow closer to God.

Fasting

Fasting is abstaining from something good and legitimate for the sake of something better and more important. In particular, fasting usually refers to limiting the ingestion of food or drink. A person fasts to imitate in some small way the sufferings of Jesus.

Fasting also is a statement that we are dependent on God for all things. Combined with prayer and other forms of mortification, fasting is a vehicle of prayer and a way to open the heart and mind to the presence and grace of God.

Fasting has always been a part of the Lenten routine of devotion. Originally the legislated fast limited the consumption of food to one meal a day during the weekdays of Lent. Also, meat and the by-products of meat animals—such as eggs, milk, and cheese—were prohibited.

The practice of eating pancakes or donuts on Shrove Tuesday (the day prior to Ash Wednesday) developed because that day was the last opportunity before Lent to enjoy foods made with milk and butter. This fast also explains the origin of the tradition of Easter eggs. After a Lent without eggs, those enjoyed on Easter tasted especially good! Of course, allowances were made for those with physical ailments or other physical limitations who could not fully participate in this fast.

Over time this Church discipline was relaxed. Eventually the assigned fast was to limit consumption of food to one main meal and two small meals per day. No food was to be eaten between meals. Today fasting is a requirement only on Ash Wednesday and Good Friday.

The regimented requirements of fasting were removed to allow the faithful more latitude in practicing mortifications that are meaningful to the individual. St. John Chrysostom once pointed out that a real fast consists not merely in abstaining from food but rather in abstaining from sin. Thus the mortifications of Lent, such as fasting, are to help the Catholic be strengthened to avoid sin.

The Church continues to call for fasting and other mortifications. However, the Church also encourages individuals to choose practices that they find personally meaningful and helpful.

Something Fishy—Abstinence

One particular form of fasting is the abstaining from meat on Fridays. At one time this was the requirement for all Fridays of the year. Now it is a practice on the Fridays in Lent.

The obvious question is "Why then is it permitted to eat fish?" According to the definition in use at the time of the regulation, meat was the flesh of warm-blooded creatures. Cold-blooded creatures such as fish, turtles, and crabs were not included because they are cold-blooded. Therefore, fish became the alternative to "meat" on days of abstinence.

Stations of the Cross

From ancient times, the places in Jerusalem associated with the Passion and death of Christ were remembered and visited. A popular devotion was to "walk the Passion with Jesus" by traveling the same route that Jesus had taken to Calvary. Along the way the individual would stop at places of significance to spend a time of prayer and reflection.

Obviously it was not possible for everyone to make the trip to Jerusalem to walk in the steps of Jesus. So during the Middle Ages the practice arose of establishing these "stations" of the Passion of Jesus in local churches. Individual stations would depict a specific scene or event from that walk to Calvary. The faithful could then use this local walk as a means of prayer and meditation on the suffering of Jesus.

Initially the number of stops for meditation and the themes of each station varied widely. By the seventeenth century the number of stations had been set at fourteen and the devotion had spread throughout Christendom.

The stations of the cross can be made at any time. Usually the individual will visit a church and walk from station to station, pausing at each for a period of prayer and meditation on some aspect of the passion of Christ. The devotion has particular significance in Lent as the faithful anticipate the celebration of Christ's Passion during Holy Week. Thus in Lent many churches conduct communal celebrations of the stations of the cross. They are normally celebrated on Fridays.

Christ directed each disciple to "take up his cross and follow" him (Mt 16:24). The stations of the cross allow the believer to do that in a literal manner, while striving to be more intimately united with Christ in his Passion.

Holy Week

Holy Week is the week that precedes the celebration of the resurrection of Jesus on Easter Sunday. It commemorates and relives those events that are pivotal to the redemptive sacrifice of Christ, by which salvation was opened to all men and women. The annual celebration of these events is quite ancient and can be easily traced back to the third century.[1]

Palm Sunday

The sixth and final Sunday of Lent is called Palm Sunday and is the beginning of Holy Week. The liturgy of the day contains four parts: the blessing of palms, a procession, Mass, and the reading of the narrative of the events from the Last Supper to the crucifixion of the Lord. This final Sunday of Lent is also called "Passion Sunday" because one of the Passion narratives from Matthew, Mark, or Luke is read.

All four evangelists tell the story of the triumphant entry of Jesus into Jerusalem prior to the annual Jewish celebration of the Passover. It is Jerusalem's version of a ticker tape-parade as crowds enthusiastically greet Jesus with shouts of "Hosanna!" (Hosanna is a Hebrew word that means "Grant salvation!")

During his public ministry, Jesus has not allowed public proclamations of himself as the Messiah—the long-awaited savior of Israel. However, for this final entry into Jerusalem, he sets the stage for an entry that fulfills the Old Testament foreshadowing of the Messiah.

Jesus dispatches two disciples to obtain a colt "on which no one has ever yet sat" (Lk 19:30). Then he enters Jerusalem on that donkey, an action that recalls the prophecy of Zechariah: "Lo, your king comes to you; triumphant and victorious is he, humble and riding on an ass, on a colt, the foal of an ass" (Zec 9:9). Jesus comes as a unique king—not one in full military honor, but rather humbly and bringing peace.

At last, Jesus allows the populace to acclaim him as the Messiah. The people give him the "red carpet treatment" by throwing their cloaks down in his path, an honor reserved for royalty. The crowd also cuts branches to spread before him.

The evangelist John identifies these as palm branches. Palm branches had long been a symbol of joy and a sign of victory. They also had a religious connotation, specifically relating to the Jewish priesthood.

Palm Sunday refocuses on that triumphant entry into Jerusalem by Jesus. Those crowds in Jerusalem were correct to honor Christ as King and Messiah, even if their understanding of the full meaning of those terms was still incomplete. On Palm Sunday, the Church celebrates Christ, the Messiah, using many of the same actions and symbols as the Gospel story, but with a clarity of meaning that is possible only in light of the death and resurrection of Christ.

Several options are available for the start of the Palm Sunday liturgy. In many instances the congregation will initially assemble at some location other than in the main church. The faithful hold palm branches as the celebrant addresses them: "Christ entered into triumph into his own city, to complete his work as our Messiah.... Let us remember with devotion this entry ... and follow him with a lively faith." The branches and the assembly are blessed with holy water,[2] and the priest prays that all present might proclaim Jesus as Messiah and King.

A procession into the church follows these prayers, with appropriate music normally accompanying the procession. The account of that first triumphant entry into Jerusalem is read from the Gospel written by the evangelist Luke. Again the Messiah is acclaimed, but now with the understanding that this king enters into his triumph through the carrying of a cross to Calvary. Those who enter the Church carrying palm branches are not only acknowledging Christ as their king and Messiah; they also are committing themselves to accompany him in his

Passion and death with the expectation of resurrection.

This perspective is accentuated as the joyful procession is soon followed with the Gospel reading from one of the three synoptic writers (Matthew, Mark, or Luke). This Gospel may be read almost as a play, with members of the congregation taking some of the different "roles." This reading reiterates that we not only remember Jesus' Passion, but we are also called to join our lives with him in his suffering and death. For, as we die in Christ, we are born to new life in his resurrection.

In the Preface of the Mass, the priest prays in the name of the entire assembled body words that sum up the meaning of this great day: "Though innocent, [Christ] accepted death to save the guilty. By his dying he has destroyed our sins."

Many people will take the blessed palms home with them as a sacramental (see chapter three). The palm can then be placed in a conspicuous place in the home—perhaps tucked around a crucifix—to serve as a reminder throughout the year of both the Passion and the kingship of Christ. The remaining palm branches are burned on Ash Wednesday, almost a year later, to anoint the heads of the faithful. This is a sign that growth in Christ and in holiness is an ongoing endeavor. The palm of rejoicing leads us back to consider our sinfulness and need for redemption.

Holy Thursday

Thursday of Holy Week begins the Paschal Triduum, the three days that are the key liturgical celebrations of the year. The institution of two sacraments, the Holy Eucharist and Holy Orders, are commemorated on this day.

Chrism Mass

In many dioceses the Chrism Mass is celebrated in the morning on Holy Thursday. This Mass is held at the cathedral of the diocese, which is the central church of the diocese and the official church of the bishop. The diocesan bishop is the celebrant of the Mass and is assisted by the other priests of the diocese as a sign of unity. During the liturgy the bishops and the priests renew their ordination commitment.

In the course of this liturgy the bishop blesses oils for use in the anointings for the sacraments of Baptism, Confirmation, and Holy Orders and in various liturgical blessings. Each parish is given some of the oil for local use. Traditionally the oil is blessed on Holy Thursday because Easter is the time when those who have been preparing to enter the Church are anointed with the holy oil as they receive the sacrament of Baptism.

Mass of the Lord's Supper

The other Mass for Holy Thursday is celebrated in the evening and is known as the Mass of the Lord's Supper. In the opening prayer of this Mass the congregation is reminded that they are gathered to celebrate the supper that Jesus left to the Church when he was preparing for his death. This supper, the Eucharist, is described as "the new and eternal sacrifice."

On that original Holy Thursday evening, Jesus and his disciples gathered, as did other pious Jews, to celebrate Passover. The Passover commemorates God's deliverance of the Hebrews from the slavery of Egypt and his leading them into the Promised Land. On Passover a spotless lamb was slain, roasted, and eaten. The blood of the lamb was smeared upon the doorposts of the houses of the faithful as a sign of God's protection. This sacrifice of the Old Covenant is described in the first reading at the Mass, from the book of Exodus (see Ex 12:1-8, 11-14).

Jesus invested the Passover of the Old Covenant with new meaning and power in the celebration of the New Covenant. He himself is the new Lamb slain for the freedom of the people. His blood is the protection from death for his followers. Christians share in the death and resurrection of Christ and experience freedom from slavery to sin and release from bondage to the power of death. A promised land is opened—a land of freedom, hope, and life with God the Father.

Institution of the Eucharist and Holy Orders

Only the original apostles were present at that first Lord's Supper. But Jesus wished that everyone would be able to partake of the "Lamb" of God who brings salvation. Therefore, although Jesus shared one meal, it would endure and be shared throughout history.

On that first Holy Thursday Jesus instituted the Eucharist as a lasting memorial. Each year the Jews celebrate a commemoration of Passover. At each Mass Catholics not only commemorate that meal, which Christ shared with the apostles, they actually participate in it.

Jesus gave himself in an unbloody manner to his disciples on Holy Thursday. He then completed that self-giving with the bloody sacrifice of Good Friday. Jesus has thus established an "unending sacrifice."[3]

The words of the institution of the sacrament of Holy Eucharist are proclaimed in the second reading of the Mass, from the first letter of Paul to the Corinthians. Jesus takes bread, breaks it, and says: "This is my body." With the wine Jesus states: "This is my blood." Christ makes the apostles into ministers, priests, of this new and everlasting covenant and sacrifice when he commands them: "Do this in remembrance of me."

Washing of Feet

The gospel for Holy Thursday is from John 13:1-15. It focuses on the unique story of Jesus' washing the feet of the disciples in the Upper Room as they begin to celebrate Passover. In the Jewish culture of the day this was a chore relegated to servants. Yet it is Jesus who undertakes the task despite the objections of Peter.

Jesus is teacher and Lord to the disciples. He is the Lamb of God, the great High Priest and the Savior of humankind who will soon be crucified. Yet he performs this humble act of love for his followers. He tells his apostles that he washes their feet as an example, and he encourages them with these words: "As I have done, so you must do."

At the Mass of the Lord's Supper, the pastor of the local church washes the feet of twelve members of the parish in imitation of Christ. This is done after the reading of the Gospel and before the Liturgy of the Eucharist.

The Mass

All the priests of the parish join in celebrating the evening Mass of Holy Thursday with the pastor as principal celebrant. Because of the solemnity of this liturgy, it is usually the only Mass celebrated in a parish on Holy Thursday. However, for pastoral reasons (such as the size of the congregation), other Masses may be added.

After the ceremony of the washing of the feet, the Mass continues as usual and is celebrated with joyful knowledge that it was on this night some two thousand years before that the Eucharist and the priesthood of the New Covenant were established. Ideally, the Gloria is sung and accompanied by music and the ringing of bells. The Gloria will then not again be sung until the Easter celebration.

Since there are no Masses on Good Friday nor on Holy Saturday, enough Hosts must be consecrated to cover the needs of those days. The Mass ends with the prayer after Communion. Following the Mass, Christ, present in the Holy Eucharist, is adored by the congregation. The Blessed Sacrament is incensed and carried in solemn procession through the church while the congregation sings a Eucharistic hymn such as *"Pange, Lingua"* ("Sing, My Tongue, the Savior's Glory").

The consecrated hosts are then taken to a side chapel or other suitable location. The main altar and the sanctuary are stripped, and crosses are covered with cloth to acknowledge that Jesus has gone to his death and burial. The Church will be redecorated to celebrate the resurrection of the Lord on Easter.

After the end of the Mass the faithful are encouraged to remain in the presence of the Lord in the temporary location. The apostles who accompanied Christ to his agony in the Garden of Gethsemane were unable to stay awake during the Lord's ordeal. So it is fitting that today's disciples would remain for a time and keep company with the Savior in the Eucharist.

Church Walk

The tradition in Rome during the Middle Ages was for the faithful to walk to the seven major churches in the city after the Mass on Holy Thursday and to pray before the Blessed Sacrament in each church. Over time the custom expanded to other parts of the Christian world and is still practiced today, although the distance between churches may necessitate use of a car.

Tenebrae

"The darkest hour," goes the old saying, "is always just before the dawn." Jesus was betrayed and seized by soldiers in the Garden of Gethsemane, scourged, crowned with thorns, ridiculed, forced to carry a cross, crucified, and buried in the tomb—dark times in which it would have seemed that the powers of darkness had triumphed. The gloom and shadows of evil seemed to predominate.

Yet this darkness soon gave way to a new dawn. Christ rose from the dead, and new light shone in our world.

Tenebrae is a Latin word for darkness. Originally the term was used to refer to the official hours of prayer that preceded the celebration of Easter. When monks would gather for their communal prayer after the

Holy Thursday liturgy and through Holy Saturday, they celebrated this time of prayer as a type of funeral service. Spiritually they traveled with Jesus in his suffering and death.

The *Tenebrae* service began with the church lighted by candles. As those in attendance prayed, the lights were slowly extinguished until darkness predominated. The other particulars of the service have varied over time, based on location and tradition.

In one tradition, a single candle is left burning but hidden behind the altar. This is the Christ candle, which at the end of the service is brought forward while the choir members bang their books to simulate an earthquake. That one light, the light of Christ, bursts forth from the tomb, dispelling the darkness and gloom.

Good Friday

Good Friday commemorates the Passion and death of Christ. From the very earliest times Christians observed each Friday of the year as a day of fasting and penance in remembrance of the day on which Christ died. The actual yearly anniversary of the Crucifixion came to be called "Good Friday."

The celebration of this feast evokes many responses: grief, awe, reverence, thankfulness, repentance, and prayer. One central liturgy for the day draws together those responses from the community of the faithful. The Liturgy of the Lord's Passion is normally celebrated at about 3:00 P.M., the hour traditionally associated with Christ's death on the cross. This liturgy is divided into three parts: the liturgy of the word, the veneration of the cross, and Holy Communion.

When the congregation arrives at the church for the service, they find a sanctuary lacking the normal ornamentation. The altar is bare. There are no flowers or decorations. The main tabernacle is empty.

The priest and the ministers enter the sanctuary in silence. It is a day to remember the death of the Lord and the fact that the sins of all men and women have made this death necessary. Upon reaching the sanctuary, the priest falls prostrate and spends a few minutes in silent prayer.

After arising, the priest goes to the presider's chair. There follows an opening prayer and the first reading, which is taken from the book of the prophet Isaiah. Many of Isaiah's writings prefigure the life, mission, and death of the Savior: "Like a lamb that is led to the slaughter ... he was taken away;... he was cut off out of the land of the living, stricken for the transgression of my people" (Is 53:7-8).

King David also prefigured Christ, and manypPsalms attributed to David foreshadow Christ, the suffering Savior. The responsorial stanza that accompanies the reading of Psalm 31 on Good Friday states: "Father, into your hands I commend my spirit." These are the final words of Jesus from the cross as he quoted this psalm (see Lk 23:46; Ps 31:5). They also become a prayer of submission to the will of God as they are spoken by the gathered congregation.

The second reading is from the Letter to the Hebrews. The writer of this epistle emphasizes the significance of Christ's death: Jesus "became the source of eternal salvation for all who obey him" (Heb 5:9).

The Passion narrative from the Gospel of John (see chapters 18–19) forms the third scriptural reading. The Passion is a drama with eternal consequences. So on Good Friday it is presented as a dramatic reading with three or four parts.

For their part, the congregation reads aloud the passages that contain words spoken by the crowds on that first Paschal Triduum. In this way, the celebration of Good Friday becomes more than a mere remembering. Each individual is invited to enter into the mystery— to see his or her place at the cross where the Savior was sacrificed.

A proper response to hearing the Word of God is prayer. Thus the readings are followed by the "General Intercessions." These prayers are similar to the prayers of intercession that normally occur at a Mass.

However, on Good Friday they take a more solemn and extended format.

Each prayer begins with a statement of the intention and an invitation to prayer. This is followed by silent prayer, which ends with the verbal formula prayer of the priest. An invitation to kneel for the time of silent prayer may be added.

Jesus died for all men and women. So the prayers cover a wide range of needs: the Church, the pope, the clergy and laity, those preparing for Baptism, the Jewish people, those who do not believe in Christ, those who do not believe in God, and the whole world.

Veneration of the Cross

St. Helena, the mother of the ancient Roman Emperor Constantine, is credited with finding the remains of the true cross of Christ in the fourth century. The practice of the solemn veneration of these relics on Good Friday began as a custom in the Jerusalem Church. A relic of the true cross was placed in a prominent location in the church, and the priest would intone: "Behold the wood of the cross."

The attention of the congregation was thus focused on the piece of wood that came from the actual cross on which Jesus died. The custom eventually spread to other areas of the Christian world. Where a relic of the original cross was unavailable, a cross or crucifix was substituted.

The veneration of the cross comes after the scriptural readings in the Good Friday liturgy. At present there are two accepted forms for the veneration.

In the first form the priest carries a cross covered by a cloth. Two acolytes with lighted candles stand on either side. The priest uncovers the upper part of the cross, elevates it, and intones: "This is the wood of the cross." The congregation responds: "Come, let us worship."

All then kneel and in silence briefly venerate the cross, which continues to be held high by the priest. This process continues two more times until the veil is removed from the cross. The cross is then taken to the sanctuary, where other ministers will hold it while the priest, other ministers, and members of the congregation come forward to perform some act of reverence to the cross. Some genuflect, some make a profound bow, and others kiss the cross.

In the second form of presentation of the cross, the priest begins at the entrance of the church. Again he is carrying the cross and is accompanied by acolytes with candles. In this form the cross is uncovered.

The priest holds it aloft and proclaims, "This is the wood of the cross." The congregation responds: "Come, let us worship." The congregation then kneels for a short period of prayer.

The priest proceeds toward the sanctuary of the church. In the middle of the church he will again raise the cross, and there will be a time of prayer. There is a final elevation when the priest reaches the sanctuary. The cross is then placed at a location where the faithful can come forward and venerate it. When the individual veneration of the cross is completed, it is placed at the altar and flanked by two candles.

The concept of veneration causes difficulty for some Protestants. They incorrectly believe that Catholics are worshiping the cross. Catholics affirm, of course, that worship is due to God alone. Through the veneration of the cross, Catholics worship God.

Consider this analogy: Many people keep a memento or photo of a family member or other loved one. They cherish that memento, give it extra care, and perhaps keep it in a special location. They don't really love that photo or memento. Rather, it is a reminder of the person whom they do love.

The principle is the same with the veneration of the cross. Since it was through Christ's death on a cross that salvation was opened to mankind, the cross has a special meaning for the Christian. It is a symbol that evokes reflection on central tenets of the faith. It draws the thoughts of the Christian to God who is the one worthy of all worship.

The cross is worthy of veneration as a sign of respect and deference.

Remember, too, as we noted earlier, that we are made of both body and soul. The two are intimately connected and only separated in death.[4] Our physical actions affect our spiritual life.

We express love of neighbor by performing acts of charity. Likewise we worship God by actions that express our worship in tangible ways. For example, we may kneel when we pray. Veneration of the cross, then, is a method of focusing our thoughts on redemption. It gives physical expression to our worship of the One who is the source of that redemption.

Holy Communion

The final part of the liturgy of Good Friday is Holy Communion. Since there is no Mass permitted on Good Friday, the Hosts have been consecrated during a previous Mass—perhaps on Holy Thursday. A cloth is placed on the altar, and the consecrated Hosts are brought to the altar along with two lighted candles. All this is done in silence and without fanfare.

The priest then begins the Communion rite by calling the congregation to pray the Our Father. The rite then proceeds as it would in an ordinary Mass. After a final prayer, all leave in silence. The altar is then again stripped.

Good Friday focuses on sorrow for our sins and a spirit of repentance. The crucifixion holds joy and hope for us, because through it and the subsequent resurrection of Christ we gain forgiveness and entrance to life. That joy and hope never leave a Christian.

Nevertheless, on Good Friday the aspects of sorrow and repentance predominate. Our sins, personal and communal, are a part of the burden that Christ carried on Calvary. In a sense, our sins are the nails that held the Savior to the cross.

We are forgiven when we repent, but it is also important to know that we are culpable. Jesus died an ignominious death. It was real and painful. Our salvation was bought at a great price. On Good Friday our focus is on the One who paid that price.

Holy Saturday

Mass may not be celebrated on Holy Saturday. It is a day of keeping vigil. Christ is in the tomb, and the faithful wait and pray.

Easter

"Jesus Christ, our King, is risen! Sound the trumpet of salvation."[5] Easter is the pivotal feast of the Church's liturgical year. In a sense, the rest of the liturgical year either prepares for and anticipates Easter, or focuses on the consequences of the Resurrection.

As St. Paul wrote: "If Christ has not been raised, then our preaching is in vain and your faith is in vain" (1 Cor 15:14). The Resurrection verifies the teaching of Christ. It affirms his divinity; it defeats sin, Satan, and death. Human history has been unalterably changed. Hope overcomes despair, and life springs from death.

It is that simple. Without the Resurrection, Christians are the most pitiable of men. Because of the Resurrection, the kingdom of God is established in power. "The Resurrection of Jesus is the crowning truth of our faith in Christ."[6] There is no doubt that, for the Catholic, Easter is the greatest feast of the liturgical year.

The celebration of the Easter Vigil begins as the sun sets on Holy Saturday. The Easter Vigil liturgy is divided into four parts: the blessing of the new fire, the liturgy of the Word, the liturgy of Baptism, and the liturgy of the Eucharist.

When the faithful arrive at the church for the Easter Vigil liturgy, they find the church dark. The focus of Good Friday and Holy Saturday has been on the death and burial of Christ. Therefore the

Lord is absent from the church, and the darkness reflects that fact.

However, a change soon occurs. A large fire is prepared, usually outside the church building. The priest, accompanied by other ministers—one of whom carries a large, unlit Easter candle—approaches the fire. The fire is blessed, and the candle is brought to the priest.

The priest cuts, or traces, a cross onto the candle with a stylus. He then traces the Greek letters *alpha* (A) and *omega* (Ω) above the cross. These are the first and last letters of the Greek alphabet—a sign that Jesus is the beginning and the end, the eternal God (see Rv 21:6). The priest may also trace the numerals of the current year on the arms of the cross, symbolically placing this point of history within the history of salvation.

During this process the priest proclaims: "Christ yesterday and today, the beginning and the end, *Alpha* and *Omega!* All time belongs to him and all ages; to him be glory and power through every age forever."

The priest then lights the candle with flame from the new fire. As fire brings light in the darkness, so in the resurrection of Christ new light has entered the world. As Jesus himself states in Scripture: "I have come as light into the world, that whoever believes in me may not remain in darkness" (Jn 12:46).

The priest prays: "May the light of Christ, rising in glory, dispel the darkness of our hearts and minds." The deacon or priest lifts the candle and proclaims, "Christ our light!" To this, all respond: "Thanks be to God!"

The ministers then process into the darkened church. All those in the church have been given candles, which until now have remained unlit. The darkness is broken as the Easter candle is again raised high.

Ministers take the light from the Paschal candle and distribute it to all the individual candles in the congregation. Soon the church is ablaze with hundreds of points of light. The light of the risen Lord has been made available to all.

The priest or deacon then carries the candle into the sanctuary. He again proclaims, "Christ our light!" as the candle is held high for a final time. The Paschal candle is placed in a stand while the deacon begins to chant the ancient hymn called the Easter Proclamation.

This prayer is known by the first Latin phrase in the hymn, *Exsultet* ("Rejoice!"). It traces the history of salvation, giving perspective to the pivotal event of the resurrection of Christ. Christ has "paid ... the price of Adam's sin." That sin is described as a "happy fault" since, because of it, the Savior became man. The hymn also calls the Easter celebration "our Passover feast" (see 1 Cor 5:7).

As we noted earlier, for Jews, Passover recalls God's deliverance of his chosen people from slavery in Egypt. A lamb was killed and eaten by the Jewish families on the eve of the beginning of the Exodus. This tradition continues to this day as Jews carry on the celebration of Passover.

For Christians, Easter is the new Passover. By it, God delivers his people from the power of Satan and death. The Lamb that is slain and becomes the food of the faithful is Jesus, the eternal Son of God.

After the chanting of the *Exsultet*, the normal lights of the Church are lit.

The Liturgy of the Word

As many as nine readings can be proclaimed during the Vigil Mass, continuing the theme of salvation history. The readings begin with the Creation story from Genesis, proceed through the calling of the patriarch Abraham, and describe how God led the Israelites through the sea while the Egyptians perished. Readings from the prophets Isaiah, Baruch, and Ezekiel speak of various aspects of the redemption that will be brought to God's people through the promised Savior.

Next, the theme of the New Testament Epistle from Romans is that of baptism, for it is through baptism that the Christian comes to "newness of life" (Rom 6:4) in the resurrection of Christ. This theme of baptism forms a transition to the next part of the liturgy.

Liturgy of Baptism

Catechumens are those taking instructions to enter the Catholic faith. Throughout Lent they study and pray in anticipation of receiving Baptism. During the Easter Vigil these catechumens are baptized and received into the Church.

The priest blesses the water that will be used in the Baptism as he dips the Easter candle into it and prays: "May all who are buried with Christ in the death of baptism rise also with him to newness of life." The baptism ceremony follows. Infants, as well as adult converts, may be baptized. Adults who are baptized will also be confirmed.

After the baptisms are completed, the entire congregation renews their baptismal vows. The priest then completes this portion of the vigil by sprinkling the congregation with baptismal water, reminding all present that they, too, have come through the waters of the sacrament into a risen, grace-filled life.

The Eucharistic Celebration

The Mass continues with the Liturgy of the Eucharist. The hymns are those of joy, for "by dying [Christ] destroyed our death; by rising he restored our life."[7]

The Masses during Easter day continue the theme of exultant joy for "the Prince of life, who died, reigns immortal."[8] In these Masses, rather than recite the creed, the congregation again renews their baptismal promises and is sprinkled with blessed water.

Customs

The customs that accompany Easter are rivaled only by those of Christmas. Some customs have secular or pagan roots. For example, the Easter rabbit is a sign of fertility and reflects new and abundant life.

Other customs have an origin more explicitly Christian in nature. For example, as we noted earlier, at one time eggs were among the foods forbidden (or used only sparingly) during Lent. So they were brought to the table on Easter and often colored red to symbolize joy. Eggs also represent new life.

Many churches practice the blessing of foods on Easter. After the long period of Lenten fasting, meats, cheeses, eggs, and special breads are brought to the church for a blessing by the priest. On the eve of Easter some Christians practice the tradition of blessing homes. This recalls the original Passover, when the angel of death bypassed the homes marked with the blood of the lamb.

Feast, Not Famine

A healthy diet requires the consumption of a variety of foods. Too much of one food group, or too little of another, can actually have an adverse effect on a person's health.

A similar principle holds for spiritual health. We need a variety of spiritual nourishment. Lent and Advent ask the faithful to focus on penance and conversion. Easter and Christmas, on the other hand, focus on joy, thanksgiving, and praise. The Church provides the liturgical cycle to encourage the right balance in our spiritual lives.

In addition to the major seasons of the year—Advent, Christmas time, Lent, Easter time, and ordinary time—other special celebrations provide the soul with a varied feast of spiritual nutrition. In popular terminology the Catholic will speak of "feast days"—the special celebrations within the Church calendar year. Actually there are four classifications of liturgical celebrations: solemnities, feasts, memorials, and optional memorials.

The life and ministry of Christ provide the framework for the entire liturgical year. Celebrations of the lives of Mary, Joseph, and the other saints spring from their relationship to Christ. The Church calendar provides these celebrations and remembrances as opportunities to grow and respond to grace.

Solemnities are the primary celebrations during the year and are celebrated with extra pomp. They include Easter and Christmas, as well as Pentecost, the Ascension, and other events from the life of our Lord. Solemnities also include various feasts of Our Lady, Mary, the Mother of Jesus. In addition, All Saints' Day (November 1), the Birth of John the Baptist (June 24), Sts. Peter and Paul (June 29), and St. Joseph's day (March 19) are also solemnities.

Other celebrations, while important, are of a lesser rank than solemnities. Days that memorialize the apostles qualify in this second rank as *feasts*. Lesser celebrations in the life of our Lord, such as the Transfiguration and the Presentation in the Temple, also qualify as feasts. All Souls' Day (November 2) is another.

Memorials occupy the lowest rank in the liturgical year. These days remember many of the saints who have faithfully lived the gospel in this life and now enjoy eternal life. Some are *obligatory* memorials, which means that the priest is to use the Mass for the celebration of the day unless it is superseded by a more important feast.

There are also *optional* memorials. On these days, the priest may choose to say either the memorial Mass or the Mass of the liturgical season. Optional memorials celebrate many saints, from Our Lady of Lourdes to St. George to St. Fidelis of Sigmaringen, among others.

Epiphany

Jesus was born a Jew, but he came to redeem all humankind. Angels, Jewish shepherds, and Gentile (non-Jewish) Magi from the East came to pay homage to the newborn King. *Epiphany* means "manifestation," and it celebrates the manifestation of the God-Man, Jesus the Savior, to the world.

This solemnity originated in the East; by the fourth century it was celebrated by the entire Church. The gospel for the day tells the story of the Magi, the wise men from the East, who followed a star to find a newborn king. They brought gifts of gold (for a king), frankincense (used by a priest), and myrrh (a fragrant perfume to anoint a body for burial). These are gifts that correspond to the ministry of Christ as King, Priest, and Savior. Jesus was born in a small Jewish town, but this feast points to the universality of his mission.

Ascension

After his resurrection, Jesus remained with his disciples for another forty days as he continued to teach and encourage them. Taking his disciples outside of Jerusalem, he gave them final directions, and then "as they were looking on, he was lifted up, and a cloud took him out of their sight" (Acts 1:9). Tradition states that the site of the Ascension was Mount Olivet. Since early Christian times the Basilica of the Ascension has stood upon Mount Olivet outside of Jerusalem.

The feast of the Ascension is celebrated on a Thursday and is a holy day of obligation for Catholics. A number of dioceses in the United States, however, now transfer the celebration to the Sunday that follows the traditional Thursday.

Jesus ascended into heaven with his glorified physical body. This is a sign and promise of the physical resurrection for all humankind at the end of time.

Pentecost

Pentecost commemorates the descent of the promised Holy Spirit upon the apostles. Before ascending to his Father, Jesus had instructed the apostles to remain in Jerusalem until the Holy Spirit, the promise of the Father, should come upon them (see Lk 24:49). Scripture states that they were gathered together in one room when "there appeared to them tongues as of fire, distributed and resting on each one of them"

(Acts 2:3). They were filled with the Holy Spirit, emboldened and empowered to go out and proclaim to the world the good news of Jesus Christ. The mission of the Church was launched!

In the Church's liturgical year this event is commemorated fifty days after Easter. The celebration can be traced back to the first century. As with many solemnities, the celebration of the feast begins with a vigil on the day prior to the feast. At the Pentecost Mass the priest wears red vestments, symbolic of the Holy Spirit and of the manifestation of "tongues of fire" on that first Pentecost.

The Mass also includes a *sequence* verse, a poetic prayer recited or sung prior to the reading of the Gospel. In Latin this poem is called *"Veni, Sancte Spiritus"*—"Come, Holy Spirit." The hymn praises the Holy Spirit and asks for his blessings and guidance: "O most blessed Light divine, shine within these hearts of yours, and our innermost being fill!... Heal our wounds, our strength renew."

The Jewish people were assembled in Jerusalem on that first Pentecost Sunday to celebrate their own feast, from which our celebration takes its name. This occasion was also known as "the Feast of Weeks" and marked the first fruits of the harvest. It also celebrated the giving of the Law to Moses on Mt. Sinai. The date for the celebration of the Jewish Pentecost was "the fiftieth day from the next day after the Sabbath of the Passover."[9]

Many customs have grown up around the celebration of Pentecost. In parts of Italy, it is the custom to scatter rose petals as a sign of the fiery tongues that accompany the arrival of the Holy Spirit. In France is a custom of blowing trumpets on Pentecost to recall "the rush of a mighty wind" (Acts 2:2) that filled the room on Pentecost. Today many people wear red to Mass on Pentecost to honor the Holy Spirit.

After many of the major feasts comes a time of liturgical celebration; for example, the weeks immediately after Easter are known as "Easter time," and each "day after Christmas" is marked for a brief season. However, after Pentecost the Church enters into what is called *ordinary time.*

With the infilling of the Holy Spirit the Church began, and now continues, her ordinary mission and life in the presence and power of the Holy Spirit. Ordinary time, for the Church, is the ongoing time of guidance by the Holy Spirit and proclamation of the Good News throughout the world.

Trinity Sunday

"Glory be to the Father, and to the Son, and to the Holy Spirit," is a familiar doxology for Catholics. The mystery of the Trinity is central to the Christian faith.

The identification of the three Persons of the Trinity can be traced through the Old Testament, the New Testament, and in the writings of the early Church fathers and ecumenical councils. Yet there was no universal celebration of this mystery until the fourteenth century. At that time Pope John XXII ordered the feast for the Latin Church.

The Sunday after Pentecost has been designated as Trinity Sunday in the Western Church. The Eastern Church continues to have no special feast to honor the Trinity.

Love is perhaps the quality most often attributed to God. We often hear repeated St. John's biblical declaration that "God is love" (1 Jn 4:8). We also know that God is eternal. Yet love only truly exists within the framework of a relationship. How then, could God be love from all eternity before he ever created angels and men to love?

We find the answer in the reality of the Trinity. God's love found expression before there were any created beings because it was expressed eternally among the three Persons of the Trinity: Father, Son, and Holy Spirit.

Early in the history of the Church various controversies arose over the nature of the Trinity. The most prominent of these concerned the heresy of Arianism in the fourth century. Arius and his followers insisted that the Son of God was created and not eternal. This heresy found many followers, especially in the Eastern Church.

The Council of Nicea in A.D. 325 settled the controversy by defining the nature of the Trinity. Belief in the Trinity had been central to the Church since the time of the apostles. As a response to Arianism, however, that belief was given a formal definition. The Church's understanding was crystallized in what we now know as the Nicene Creed, which states:

> We believe in one God, the Father, the Almighty.... We believe in one Lord, Jesus Christ, the only Son of God, eternally begotten of the Father, God from God, Light from Light, true God from God ... one in Being with the Father.... We believe in the Holy Spirit, the Lord, the giver of life, who proceeds from the Father and the Son. With the Father and the Son he is worshiped and glorified.

The Council of Nicea explained that there were three persons in the Trinity, but only one being. The three persons are equal and of the same substance (that is, *consubstantial*). All three persons are eternal and are to be worshiped.

The Council provided definition and clarity in the midst of controversy. However, the Trinity still remains a mystery beyond the ability of the human mind to fathom. Trinity Sunday provides an opportunity for Catholics to affirm the doctrine and to honor God as Trinity.

This Mass also invites us to enter into the mystery and partake of the grace God offers. One of the prayers for Trinity Sunday speaks in these words to God: "You reveal yourself in the depths of our being, drawing us to share in your life and love."[10] Each man and woman is invited to share in that eternal Trinitarian love.

Corpus Christi

The Thursday after Trinity Sunday was traditionally celebrated as Corpus Christi—the Feast of the Body and Blood of Christ. In 1970, with the release of a New Roman Missal, the Vatican gave permission to move this feast from Thursday to the following Sunday. Thus some countries continue to celebrate the Feast of the Body and Blood of Christ on a Thursday, while others celebrate on the following Sunday. In the United States this feast falls on the Sunday after Trinity Sunday.

Corpus Christi focuses on the institution of the Eucharist at the Last Supper that Jesus shared with his disciples on the Thursday prior to his crucifixion. As we have noted, from that time forward, whenever a valid Mass is offered, bread and wine are changed into the Body and Blood of Christ. This "transubstantiation"[11] occurs when the priest says the words: "This is my Body.... This is my Blood" as commanded by Jesus at the Last Supper.

The bread and wine are truly and irrevocably changed at that time. Jesus becomes present—Body, Blood, Soul, and Divinity—upon the altar. He offers himself as spiritual food to the faithful.

The Hosts that remain after the faithful receive Communion are transferred to a secure place, typically a tabernacle. Jesus remains present in the Eucharist under the appearance of the bread. During the Middle Ages it became a common practice for the faithful to visit Christ in the tabernacle outside of Mass and spend time in prayer and worship.

In the year 1264, Pope Urban IV established the Feast of Corpus Christi as an annual celebration of the great and wonderful gift of the Eucharist. He also commissioned the great theologian, St. Thomas Aquinas, to compose hymns and prayers specifically for this celebration. In obedience to the request of the Holy Father, Thomas composed some of the most beautiful and profound Eucharistic poems the Church possesses.

The sequence that can be used at the Mass of Corpus Christi was composed by St. Thomas. Although the beauty of the Latin cannot be adequately captured in a translation, nonetheless even in English the mystery of the Eucharist is conveyed:

Here in outward signs are hidden
Priceless things, to sense forbidden;
Signs, not things, are all we see:
Flesh from bread, and Blood from wine;
Yet is Christ, in either sign,
All entire confessed to be.

They too who of him partake
Sever not, nor rend, nor break,
But entire their Lord receive.
Whether one or thousands eat,
All receive the selfsame meat,
Nor the less for others leave.[12]

During the Protestant Reformation many concepts of the Eucharist were challenged. Initially Martin Luther accepted a traditional belief in the Eucharist, although he stated that the "real presence" of Christ (as it is traditionally called) was only at the moment of reception and not afterwards. Other reformers went even further and proclaimed only a "spiritual" presence of Christ.

The Council of Trent in the sixteenth century reaffirmed the Church's belief in the real presence and adopted the word "transubstantiation." The Council cited the long Tradition of belief in this reality that was traceable back to the early Church. The Council also pointed to a traditional understanding of the Scriptures. One relevant scriptural text is found in the Gospel of John where Christ tells his followers: "Truly, truly, I say to you, unless you eat the flesh of the Son of man and drink his blood, you have no life in you" (Jn 6:53).

Processions and Celebrations

The real presence of Christ in the Eucharist is a great source of comfort to the Catholic. Christ is close and available to give life, solace, and grace. Eucharistic devotions, such as Benediction of the Blessed Sacrament (that is, of the Eucharist), have long been a part of Church life.

The truth of the Eucharist is also a source of joy—a joy and truth that are too wonderful to keep hidden. For that reason, on the Feast of Corpus Christi it is an old tradition to process through public streets with a priest carrying the Blessed Sacrament in a monstrance.[13] The faithful participate in the procession while singing Eucharistic hymns. This reverent procession, in essence, takes Christ literally to the greater community. Many countries, such as Poland, continue the custom of solemn processions on the Feast of Corpus Christi, and in some American cities the custom is being revived.

The Sacred Heart of Jesus

When you hear the word *heart*, what comes to mind? Perhaps the physical human heart, or—what has long been symbolized by the heart—love. When considering devotion to the Sacred Heart of Jesus, those two concepts are important.

To speak of the physical heart of Jesus, a part of the whole God-Man, is to consider the person of Jesus. Thus to speak of the heart of Jesus is to speak of Jesus.

We regularly use the word *heart* in this way when we speak of the person. For example, to say, "My heart goes out to him," means that as a person, I have concern for someone else.

If a young man sends a card to his girlfriend decorated with a stylized picture of a heart, she will have no difficulty deciphering the meaning of that card. "Heart" in our culture connotes love. Not surprisingly, then, the emblem of the Sacred Heart of Jesus symbolizes his love for each person.

So, devotion to the Sacred Heart is a means of focusing on Jesus and the love that he manifests. Yet there is another part of the traditional symbol of the Sacred Heart. That emblem shows the heart pierced by a dagger.

Jesus has loved us to the fullest, giving his life freely on the cross. Yet his love has often gone unrequited. Even Christians fail to respond to his love by continuing to embrace sin in their lives. So Christ's heart is pierced because of a lack of response to his love.

The Feast of the Sacred Heart focuses attention both on the great love of the Son of God and on the lack of love of those who are called to follow him. The solemnity gives an opportunity for Catholics both to thank God and to make reparation for sins and failings.

Private devotion to the Sacred Heart can be traced back to the eleventh and twelfth centuries. The devotion became more popular and well-known in the seventeenth century when a French Visitandine nun, St. Margaret Mary Alacoque, received a series of revelations. In these revelations our Lord asked that devotion to his Sacred Heart be fostered.

Jesus specifically asked that Catholics make frequent Communions, in particular for reparation (that is, making amends for wrongdoing) for the many wounds inflicted on his heart through the lack of responsive love to him. St. Margaret Mary stated that our Lord wished the faithful to receive Communion on First Fridays specifically in reparation. The Friday after the feast of Corpus Christi was also to be celebrated in honor of his Sacred Heart.

It is interesting to note that many other saints of the seventeenth century were promoting devotion to the Sacred Heart. Among these were St. John Eudes, St. Francis Borgia, St. Aloysius, and others. Initially, permission to celebrate the feast was only granted to the

Visitandine Sisters. Then in 1856 Pope Pius IX declared that the Feast of the Sacred Heart was to be celebrated by the universal Church.

The Solemnity of the Sacred Heart of Jesus is celebrated on the Friday after the Second Sunday after Pentecost. The theme and prayers of the Mass continue to focus on the double intention of love and reparation: "Father, we honor the heart of your Son broken by man's cruelty, yet symbol of love's triumph, pledge of all that man is called to be. Teach us to see Christ in the lives we touch, to offer him living worship by love-filled service...."[14]

Family Consecration to the Sacred Heart

Perhaps you have seen a picture or statue of the Sacred Heart in a Catholic home. If so, it is likely that the family has been consecrated to the Sacred Heart. Consecration means to "make holy."

Such a family seeks to dedicate itself to Christ and to live holy and righteous lives through his gracious presence in the family. By their devotion and commitment to the Sacred Heart, the family seeks to make reparation for the many instances in which Christ has been ignored in the world. The picture or statue is usually placed in a prominent location in the home and serves as a constant reminder that Christ is present as the unseen guest of that family.

The Assumption

Where is the burial place of the Mother of Jesus? Historians and archaeologists can point to the burial locations of various apostles and early martyrs. Often churches were built over the graves of revered saints. A very early Christian church built outside the walls of Old Jerusalem was identified as the location where Mary died. However, it was not identified as the location of Mary's grave.

Instead, this church was known as the Church of the Dormition of Mary—that is, the place where Mary "fell asleep." From very early times Christians proclaimed that when Mary died her physical body did not remain on earth. Physically and spiritually she was "assumed" into heaven.

The feast of the Assumption, which is celebrated every August 15, commemorates the fact that Mary was physically taken into heaven. From the writings of early Church fathers it can be demonstrated that this feast was celebrated in Palestine by the year 500. The Assumption was an accepted fact in the Church throughout its history. However, it was only in November of 1950 that the Assumption was formally and infallibly proclaimed as a dogma of the Church. This proclamation was not of a new belief; rather, it was a solemn affirmation of a Tradition that had been handed down from generation to generation from earliest times.

The Second Vatican Council in the document *Lumen Gentium* reaffirmed the dogma of the Assumption: "the Immaculate Virgin ... was taken up body and soul into heaven, when her earthly life was over."[15] In the normal course of events, the physical bodies of men and women undergo decay after death. This is an effect of original sin. However, Mary was free of original sin.[16] Therefore her body did not undergo the normal process of decay.

The Assumption is also a sign of hope for all humankind. Christ, through his Passion, death, and resurrection, has triumphed over sin and death. Additionally, Christ is restoring the original order and intent of creation. Therefore, at the end of time a new heaven and a new earth will be established (see 2 Pt 3:13; Rv 21:1). Our souls will be reunited with our bodies in a glorified state. Mary is the first recipient of that promise's fulfillment.

All Saints' Day
Heaven is full of unsung heroes, men and women who have responded to God's grace and sought to follow Christ in this life. Some of these

unrecognized saints lived quiet and holy lives that may have been noticed by only a few. Others repented on their deathbed of a life of sin and asked God to wash them clean and receive them as his children.

Many saints are recognized by the Church as definitely being in heaven. These canonized[17] saints are placed before us as examples of sanctity—men and women who can serve as inspiration and models. However, the canonized saints are only the tip of the iceberg. For every canonized saint there are probably thousands of uncanonized saints.

How can we say that with any degree of assurance? It is because of the mercy of God. It is Christ's desire that all should respond, receive forgiveness and grace, and ultimately enjoy the fruits of eternal life. What percentage of all those who have lived upon the earth are now in heaven? What percentage have rejected God's free gift and have chosen hell? We cannot know those numbers in this life.

In the early Church it was the custom to remember a martyr on the anniversary of his or her martyrdom. Under the reign of the Emperor Diocletian, the number of those martyred for the faith increased significantly. Literally there were too many martyrs to be able to remember them individually.

For that reason, a day was established to honor them corporately—All Saints' Day. Thus the celebration of All Saints' Day can be traced back as early as the fourth century. In the eighth century Pope Gregory III set the annual day to honor the saints as November 1.

As with many solemnities, the evening prior to the actual feast is celebrated as a vigil—a time to prepare for the celebration. The night prior to All Saints' Day is one such vigil and was known in earlier times as "All Hallows' ["Hallows" means "Saints"] Eve." From this name we derive the term "Halloween."

On the vigil of All Saints', children would dress as various saints. Small gifts, such as fruit or sweets, would be distributed as part of the celebration. Unfortunately, the vigil of All Saints' Day has lost its religious significance. However, some Christians have made an effort to recapture the original meaning by conducting "All Saints' Parties" to replace the secular "trick or treat" activities.

Why Celebrate the Saints?

All Saints' Day is only one of many celebrations throughout the Church's liturgical year that recalls various saints. The Church has several reasons for including these feasts in the liturgical year.

First, we should note that ultimately, men and women merit heaven because of the mercy and grace of God. The holiest person who has ever lived could not have merited heaven without the redeeming work of Christ. Even Mary, the Mother of God, needed the salvation offered through Christ. So to honor the saints is fundamentally to honor Christ.

The life of each saint is in some way a reflection of Christ. No saint would boast that he or she had attained holiness by personal effort alone. St. Paul spoke on behalf of all the saints when he said that he would boast only of Christ (see 1 Cor 1:31; 2 Cor 10:17). Actually, saints boast of their weakness, as St. Paul did (see 2 Cor 12:9), because through it God shows his mercy and strength. To look at a saint is to see the God he or she serves and worships.

The Church also honors saints because it encourages us to look at saints as examples and models. Their sanctity was a result not only of God's grace but also of their response to that grace. Canonized saints are outstanding examples of men and women who generously responded to the call and grace of God.

Many saints responded in heroic proportion. Some lived lives of outstanding service, while others used their skills to proclaim the gospel in foreign lands. Many saints lived humble lives of prayer and repentance. Still others followed the example of their Lord and gave their lives as martyrs for the faith.

The saints have come from a variety of ethnic, social, and economic backgrounds. They have hailed from Africa and Asia, the Americas and Europe. There are saints who were paupers and saints who were kings and queens.

Saints were of all personality types as well. St. Philip Neri and St. John Bosco were renowned for their jokes, pranks, and sense of humor. St. Catherine of Siena, on the other hand, was of a choleric temperament. Some saints struggled regularly with anger. Others were tempted often by lust.

Nevertheless, all the saints have one thing in common: They gave their lives to God and sought to follow his will in all circumstances. So no matter what a person's temperament, education, social standing, or predominant weakness, that person can probably identify a saint who shared in his or her difficulties and can serve as a model and inspiration.

Praying to the Saints

Though God's grace is always available, he is also a perfect gentleman. He doesn't force his will or his gifts upon people; he waits for us to ask. Christians believe that when they ask him, God hears the prayers of his people.

Prayer is effective because it establishes a relationship with God that allows him to work in the life of an individual. Prayer opens the doors of grace. And we can pray not only for our needs but also for the needs of others. So Christians will often ask others to pray for them.

In addition, all Christian believers are united in the body of Christ (see Rom 12:5 and 1 Cor 12:12). We are interconnected under Christ the Head. Our actions, good or bad, affect the other members of the body. If I draw closer to God and if I am more faithful to God's will for my life, that has a positive effect on other Christians.

Christianity has a personal dimension: I can relate to God personally as an individual. However, Christ also emphasized the corporate nature of Christianity. He established a Church, a communion of believers, and he works with us as a people. So I can become a conduit of God's grace to other people and a help to God's work in the world. When I ask another Christian to intercede for me, I am tapping into a wider network of the body of Christ.

Now Christ, the Head, has only one body. Thus it must be that his body includes those now living and those who have died and share in his eternal life—that is, the saints. If I can ask my neighbor on earth to pray for me, I can also ask my neighbor in heaven to pray for me, because we are all united in Christ.

What is more, the saints in heaven have a closer relationship with Christ than Christians who continue with the struggles of life here on earth. The heavenly members of the body of Christ have been purified and are completely submitted to the will of God. They stand before the throne of God and see him "face to face" (see 1 Cor 13:12).

For this reason, they can be pure channels of God's grace. Certainly their prayers are effective. Scripture tells us that the prayers of the saints are like "golden bowls full of incense" (Rv 5:8) before the throne of God. Not surprisingly, then, in addition to honoring the saints and imitating their example, Catholics also ask for the saints' intercession.

All Souls' Day

Christ's followers exist in one of three states. Those reading this book, for example, are experiencing life on the earth. Traditionally, we earth-bound believers are called the *Church Militant*. We are struggling to live faithful lives as followers of Christ. We "fight the good fight of the faith" (1 Tm 6:12) with the hope of heaven in the future.

A second division of the followers of Christ is the *Church Triumphant*. These are believers who have died and now enjoy eternal life with God in heaven.

However, some believers make up yet a third category of membership in the body of Christ. This group encompasses those who have died in a relationship with Christ—in the state of grace—but who were not ready to come fully into God's presence. These believers are known as the *Church Suffering* because they are undergoing a time of purification before entry into heaven. As we have already noted, this time of purification has traditionally been identified as *purgatory*.

Why do some (perhaps most) followers of Christ need this time of purification? Because God is all-holy, and nothing impure can exist in his presence.

It's true, of course, that we achieve salvation through the effective and saving work of Christ. No one, no matter how good, can merit heaven in his or her own right. Without Christ there is no salvation.

Nevertheless, we all respond to the grace of Christ in varying degrees. Most of us continue to struggle with sin. We gain forgiveness through Christ, but the Church tells us that even though we are forgiven, there remains a *temporal punishment* as a consequence of our sins.

One often-used analogy to clarify the need for purgatory is that of a man who commits suicide by jumping off a twenty-story building. On the way down he sincerely repents of his sin. God hears and forgives the man. However, there still will be some very unpleasant consequences when he hits the ground! Our sin has consequences other than guilt, and these consequences are our temporal punishment—temporal because they only last for a time rather than for eternity.

Another way to think about purgatory is to recall that Scripture speaks of our being like gold refined in fire (see Mal 3:2-3). When gold is purified, the dross is burned off so that only pure metal remains. Historically, the punishment of purgatory has been described as fire (see 1 Cor 3:12-15). It is a fire that purifies the soul, removing attachments to the world so that the soul can be attached to God alone in heaven.

All Souls' Day is celebrated on November 2, and is a commemoration of all the faithful departed. It reminds the faithful on earth to pray for those souls in purgatory. Since the Mass is the most perfect and effective form of prayer, the Mass of All Souls' Day is offered specifically for the souls of the faithful departed.

The practice of praying for departed believers goes back to the beginning of Christianity. The practice of a specific day dedicated to praying for "all souls" developed over time.

Christ the King

Even though few countries today are still governed by kings, we continue to understand the concept. Kings are typically powerful men who rule from golden thrones with pomp and pageantry.

The Scripture identifies Christ as the "King of kings" (see Rv 17:14), but he is not a typical king. Jesus is a king whose throne is the cross.

When Pilate, the Roman governor, asked Jesus if he were a king, Jesus answered: "You have said so" (Mt 27:11). Shortly after that conversation, Pilate handed Jesus over to be crucified. The description of the crime that was placed on the placard above Christ on the cross read: "This is Jesus, the King of the Jews" (Mt 27:37).

The kingship of Jesus is not like the kingship of other men. Jesus himself stated that his kingdom was not of this world (see Jn 18:36); yet he truly is King. In fact, the Book of Revelation identifies the risen Christ as "the ruler of kings" (Rv 1:5).

The Solemnity of Christ the King provides a fitting end to the Church's liturgical year. It is celebrated on the last Sunday of the year, before the beginning of Advent. This feast provides an occasion to honor Christ, who is enthroned in heaven and will come back on the clouds at the end of time.

Jesus also desires to rule in the hearts of men and women, but he only does so when invited. Thus this feast offers an opportunity for each individual to make Christ the Lord of his or her life. By extension the Church prays that all men and women would acknowledge Christ as King. When Christ fully rules in the world it will be "a kingdom of truth and life, a kingdom of holiness and grace, [and] a kingdom of justice, love, and peace."[18]

The Immaculate Conception

In December of 1854 Pope Pius IX issued an authoritative, infallible definition of a dogma. He wrote that the Blessed Virgin Mary "in the first instance of her conception, by a singular privilege and grace granted by God, in view of the merits of Jesus Christ, the Savior of the human race, was preserved exempt from all stain of original sin."[19]

As a rule, all men and women come into this world with original sin. It is a part of the human condition, a consequence of the initial sin and fall of the first humans. But there are exceptions to this rule. One is Eve, the first woman created by God. She was born without the effects of original sin and with a fully free will.

Eve, along with her husband, Adam, rebelled against God by rejecting his commands. Since that original sin, humankind has experienced the consequences of that act. Just as science informs us that everyone receives a genetic imprint from his or her predecessors, our faith tells us that everyone also receives the spiritual imprint of original sin through our original parents.

Nevertheless, Pius IX, speaking for the entire Church, states that, like Eve, Mary did not start out with that imprint, that stain, of sin. Pope Pius stressed that the Mother of Jesus—who was therefore the Mother of God—was free from sin from the very moment of her conception.

The obvious question is "How is that possible?" After all, Mary was conceived in the same manner as every other person after Eve: by the sexual intercourse of two human parents. Pope Pius explained why Mary was exempt when he stated that this miracle was through "a singular privilege and grace granted by God, in view of the merits of Jesus Christ."

Every Catholic is cleansed of original sin through the grace of Baptism. That grace is available through the One who established the sacrament of Baptism, Jesus Christ. The effects of original sin have been overcome through the death and resurrection of Christ. So each Catholic gains a certain freedom by Baptism.

Mary was spared from being conceived in original sin by the same grace, through the saving work of Christ. She was kept sinless, not because of her parents and not through any action of her own, but rather by the grace of Jesus Christ. As the opening prayer of the Mass puts it on the feast of the Immaculate Conception: "Father, you let [the Virgin Mary] share *beforehand* in the salvation Christ would bring by his death, and kept her sinless from the first moment of her conception."

Some will still question: But how can this be possible if Mary was born before Christ's death on the cross? It is helpful to remember that even though as humans we are defined by time, God is eternal. For God there is no yesterday and no tomorrow. Though divine timelessness is a concept shrouded in mystery, the truth is that time is no barrier to the work of Christ.

The Immaculate Conception is a dogma that was only officially promulgated in recent times. However, the development of the dogma can be seen over time. For example, from the earliest centuries Mary was identified as the "new Eve"—the first woman who was free from original sin. Many of the Church fathers, such as Justin, Irenaeus, Tertullian, and others, used this title for Mary.

The purity of Mary was also a regular topic in the preaching and writing of the early Church fathers. St. Ambrose (fourth century), for example, says that Mary was "incorrupt, a virgin immune through grace from every stain of sin" (see his "Sermon on Psalm 118"). Other early writers echoed this thought.

Scripture scholars have also noted the term "full of grace," the salutation given by the angel to Mary at the Annunciation (see Lk 1:28). How could Mary be "full of grace" if she was tainted by original sin? This greeting points to the fact of the Immaculate Conception.

Nonetheless, it was not until the fifteenth century that the concept of the Immaculate Conception took on a more formal definition in the life of the Church. The final formulation and definition was then provided by Pope Pius IX in 1854, who declared that the entire Church should celebrate the Feast of the Immaculate Conception on every December 8.

From Advent to Christ the King Sunday, we can see, then, how the cycle of the Church's annual liturgical calendar allows Catholics to enter into the mystery of Christ's redemption. Each season, each feast, becomes an opportunity for believers to grow in grace and in fellowship with the saints who await us close to the heart of God.

Sacramentals and Signs

Sacraments give grace. Sacramentals give grace? The first sentence is a declarative statement; the second is a question. Together they reflect the major difference between a sacrament and a sacramental. A sacrament most certainly gives grace; we can declare that truth with assurance. But we cannot be so certain about whether a sacramental gives grace on a particular occasion. That's an open question, depending on several circumstances.

What exactly is a *sacramental*? A sacramental is a sacred sign that possesses a likeness to the sacraments and whose effects are obtained by the prayer of the Church. Sacramentals can be objects, such as holy water, medals, rosaries, or ashes, or they can be actions, such as a blessing. When sacramentals are "things," they are often blessed and dedicated by a minister of the Church. When they are blessings, they are initiated by the prayers of a minister of the Church.

How Sacramentals Differ From Sacraments

As we have noted, there are seven sacraments. There will never be more, nor will there be fewer. Christ instituted the seven sacraments, and they are effective instruments for providing grace. Grace is bestowed through a sacrament regardless of the worthiness of the minister or the recipient.

In short, sacraments have God's guarantee. They give grace—period. Now, the effect of sacraments on particular individuals can vary depending on the receptivity of the individual. If the person is already in the state of grace, is open, and is prayerful, then he or she is in a good position for grace to be effective. But the converse is also true. If someone is hard of heart and lacking faith, even though grace is present through the sacrament it may not be very effective in the individual.

I can give you a hammer so you can pound nails into wood and build something of value. But I can't force you to use that hammer. If you choose, you can set it aside and try to install the nails with your bare hands!

It's the same way with the grace of the sacrament. God gives the grace. But the individual will choose whether and to what degree to use that grace.

While all this is true of sacraments, sacramentals differ from them in several ways. First, while the sacraments were instituted by Christ, sacramentals are instituted by the Church. So the number of sacramentals can change. New types of sacramentals can be added by the Church, while others can fall into disuse in the life of the Church.

Second, sacramentals can be a source of grace for the individual, but there are no guarantees of grace as there are for sacraments. The grace that a person receives from the use of a sacramental will depend on the disposition of the individual.

For example, on Ash Wednesday, the priest blesses ashes and distributes them on the foreheads of the faithful. That process may have absolutely no effect on an individual, or it may be a source of blessing and grace. It depends primarily on the disposition of the individual. If someone receives ashes with the desire to enter Lent as a time of repentance, and if he or she approaches the reception of the ashes with an attitude of heart that is open to God, the reception can provide grace and strengthen the individual so that he or she can better respond to God's call.

If sacramentals depend on the disposition of the individual, then why bother? Why not just ask God personally and directly for help and actual grace? The use of the sacramental has extra benefit because the prayer of the entire Church is invoked by the use of the sacramental.

Consider this parallel from banking. Someone with a checking account can draw money from the bank for various needs. But imagine that the same individual is given access to all the money available through the Federal Reserve Bank. He or she could have quite a shopping spree with those resources!

The principle is similar with sacramentals. Yes, I can and I should ask God to give me grace to fulfill my responsibilities and live a worthy life. However, by using a sacramental with the right disposition, I tap into the grace available in and through the Church.

When a minister of the Church blesses a sacramental, the blessing of that object contains a prayer for the person who uses that item. So, for example, when someone uses holy water that has been blessed, and uses it with a proper disposition, the prayer of the Church is extended to that individual.

Have you seen any of those old Dracula movies on late night television? The hero often shows a crucifix to drive away Dracula. That fictional scenario does have a basis in truth. Sacramentals are not only a source of grace to live a holy life; they also can be a source of protection against the work of the devil.

In this regard it is important first to note that evil does exist and that there are evil spirits—fallen angels who have rebelled against God. The devil "prowls around like a roaring lion, seeking some one to devour" (1 Pt 5:8). Given that reality, sacramentals can help in the defense against the attacks of the devil.

Remember, though, that sacramentals do not grant grace automatically. So merely having holy water or a crucifix does not guarantee anything. The belief that the mere possession of a sacramental has an automatic effect is a superstition.

On the other hand, to use a sacramental with the right disposition can be a great help in combating the attack of evil. So the person who struggles with temptation can ask God's help and also utilize a sacramental, such as making the sign of the cross with holy water. The prayers of the individual are then combined with the prayer of the Church through the sacramental. Grace is made available in abundance to stand against the temptation.

Certain other objects and actions in addition to sacramentals can be helpful to the believer because they act as signs that encourage piety and devotion. These may be objects that have not been specifically blessed—perhaps a card with a picture of the Sacred Heart of Jesus used as a bookmark—or an action, such as bowing toward the altar in church. Such objects and actions help a person recollect and focus in prayer or meditation.

Holy Water

In nature, water is essential to life. Water is a vehicle for the spiritual transmission of grace and new life in Christ.

As we have noted, the grace of Baptism is conferred through the words of the baptismal rite and the use of water. Baptism is the sacrament of initiation that removes sin and brings an individual into the body of Christ. In the early Church the normal time for Baptism to be administered was at the Easter Vigil. Water would be blessed at the Easter Vigil so that Baptism could be administered to the catechumens.

We have historical evidence that by the fourth century water was used outside of Baptism as a sacramental. For example, during the Easter season blessed water was used to sprinkle those who had already been baptized, as a reminder of their own Baptism and as an opportunity to renew their baptismal promises. This notion of sprinkling with water has a New Testament precedent: "Let us draw near with a true heart in full assurance of faith, with our hearts sprinkled clean from an evil conscience and our bodies washed with pure water" (Heb 10:22).

In the Old Testament as well, water had often been used in various ceremonies in the temple as a sign of cleansing from impurities and as part of the ritual of repentance. Water was also used in the blessing of items being dedicated for use in the temple worship.

In Christian tradition, believers would take the blessed water from the church to their homes and use it in family situations to bless foods and those suffering from illness. The water's connection with the life-giving properties of Baptism encouraged its use this way. In addition, the blessed water, when used in a prayerful context, helped Christians to drive away evil spirits or resist temptation.

Today, holy water continues to be used in a variety of liturgical services. For example, in the funeral liturgy holy water is used in the prayers for the deceased. The water may be sprinkled on the casket as the prayers of the funeral rite are said. In death, the believer enters into eternal life. The connection of holy water with the waters of Baptism focuses attention on the saving grace of Christ and on that hope of eternal life in him.

When objects are blessed and dedicated for liturgical use, holy water is often used in the ceremony as a sign of cleansing and consecration—just as the waters of baptism cleanse the individual and consecrate the person to God. Holy water is also used to bless the rings exchanged in a marriage ceremony. This blessing is a sign of the connection of the two sacraments: Baptism brings life to the individual, and Matrimony makes two into one, bringing new life through children and a new witness of love to the world.

At the doors of most Catholic churches is a bowl containing holy water. Upon entering the church, Catholics dip their fingers into the water and make a sign of the cross. "In the name of the Father and of the Son and of the Holy Spirit" is part of the baptismal formula. As we enter the church, then, it is an appropriate time to recall Baptism, to remember that through those waters we have entrance into the presence and grace of God.

Many Catholics today continue to use holy water at home. All Christians have received a priestly ministry through Baptism, and parents in particular have the responsibility to pass the faith on to their children. Part of that parental and priestly role is to pray for and bless the children. So the sprinkling of the children with water ties this particular parental ministry to the prayers and ministry of the entire Church. Also, when someone is sick, the family can accompany the prayers of the household with the sprinkling of holy water, thus joining their prayers to the prayers and blessing of the whole Church.

Holy water, as with any sacramental, can be used in a superstitious manner. The water has no magical power, but combined with prayer and an attitude of reliance on Christ's grace, it does provide a means of conveying grace. In this way God uses ordinary substances and ordinary people dedicated to him as a conduit of grace.

Statues, Icons, and Christian Art

The visual arts can help us focus on profound realities that transcend our daily lives. So the Church has long used art as a means to convey spiritual and supernatural truth.

The catacombs—underground tunnels that served as the burial places of early Christians—are decorated with many paintings on the walls and some items of sculpture. Some depict martyrs or display the cross. Other depictions are more symbolic, such as a fish. (The letters of the Greek word for "fish" correspond to the initials in the Greek words of the phrase "Jesus Christ, Son of God, Savior.")

Christian art has continued to play an important role in Catholic worship. Some art is stylized or symbolic. For example, the towering spires of the Gothic cathedral are intended to lift the eyes of the viewer toward the heavens, and so also to lift the thoughts and the spirit toward the things of God. Other images depict our Lord, his mother, or the saints.

Catholics *venerate* (show reverence to) these sacred images. This veneration is focused on the person whom the art represents. The *Catechism of the Catholic Church* is clear on this point: "The Christian veneration of images is not contrary to the first commandment which proscribes idols. Indeed, 'the honor rendered to an image passes to its prototype,' and 'whoever venerates an image venerates the person portrayed in it.'"[1]

A parallel can be found in parents who carry pictures of their children in their purse or wallet. They don't love the pictures; they love the children shown in the photographs. Those photographs provide a tangible link to their family when they are not physically present.

Christian art can be found in churches and other places of public worship, as well as in homes, places of business, and places set aside for private devotion. When the statue or other piece of art is installed in a church, it is usually blessed specifically as a sacramental. The prayers that accompany such a blessing focus not so much on the statue as on the person represented by the statue.

For example, when blessing the statue of a saint, the minister prays: "He (she) [that is, the saint whom the statue represents] is for us a witness to the life of the gospel and stands in your presence to plead for us. Grant that we may benefit from his (her) intercession."[2] This prayer points to two important reasons for the use of a sacred image: witness and prayer.

Students from across America visit the statue of Abraham Lincoln in the Lincoln Memorial in Washington. As they look at the memorial and read the words inscribed in the granite, they may feel inspired. Feelings of patriotism and a desire for justice are common sentiments experienced by those who visit.

Christian art should have a similar effect. Viewing a statue or painting of the Blessed Mother is an opportunity to meditate on her complete trust and obedience to God. Her heroic life can inspire and encourage those who see the artwork or memorial to Mary and reflect on the meaning of her life.

Christian artwork is also an aid to prayer. It is easy to lose focus during prayer, with distractions seemingly overpowering at times. Christian artwork can provide a focus that assists in overcoming distractions and stirs positive contemplation.

For example, to pray before a crucifix reminds the believer that Christ suffered and died for all men and women. To behold his pain calls forth a sense of sorrow and repentance for personal sin. Prayers of love and thankfulness can rise from hearts to God.

The media and styles of Christian art vary widely, with clear distinctions between the art of the Western and Eastern Churches. In the West, art has traditionally tended toward realism. Artists attempted to depict our Lord and the saints as they may have looked while on earth. Sculpture was highly prized because the three-dimensional approach added to the sense of realism.

The Eastern Church, on the other hand, has adopted a very different approach. Traditionally, Eastern artists and artisans have not sought realism. Eastern statuary is rarely found. Instead, the art of the Eastern Church seeks to convey heavenly realities. The art is more stylized and serves as "windows into heaven."

Instead of realistic statues, the Eastern Church produced *icons*. These are flat images in which every detail of color, shape, and object has a meaning. Icons are a means to teach and encourage thoughts of heavenly realities that transcend the earthly.

The Rosary

The most popular private devotion among Catholics may well be the *rosary*. The rosary is both a form of prayer and a specific sacramental that aids in prayer.

The physical object that Catholics call a rosary is a looped string of beads. The traditional rosary has five sets of ten beads spaced closely together. Before each set of ten is a single bead set off from the others. At the head of the loop is a short string of four beads with one set off from the other three beads. A crucifix is at the head of this string.

Praying the rosary involves recitation of common prayers while meditating on various events, called mysteries, associated with the life of Christ. There are twenty of these mysteries, divided into four sets of five: joyful, luminous, sorrowful, and glorious.

To pray the rosary, a Catholic starts by reciting the Apostles' Creed. This statement of belief both affirms the faith of the one praying and sets the background for prayer. The prayer that follows is not aimless; rather it is focused on the realities expounded in the creedal statement.

The Creed is followed by the recitation of an "Our Father," three "Hail Marys," and the doxology commonly called the "Glory Be." These are among the first prayers Catholic parents teach their children.

The *Our Father* is the prayer taught by Jesus to his disciples. This single composition includes several prayers of adoration, contrition, and petition. They provide rich material for meditation and reflection.

The *Hail Mary* both pays honor to the Mother of God and asks for her intercession. In effect, the repetition of the Hail Mary while meditating on the mysteries is asking Mary to intercede with her Son that the realties of the mysteries would find a home in the life, thoughts, and witness of the person who is praying the rosary. Scripture says that Mary reflected on the mysteries of the life and mission of her Son, "pondering them in her heart" (Lk 2:19). The rosary is a means to join

Mary in her "pondering" and by this means draw closer to the Son of God.

The final prayer of this initial part of the rosary is the *Doxology*, which is an utterance of praise to the Trinity.

The initial prayers of the rosary are often said for the intention of the increase of faith, hope, and love in the life of the individual. This introductory prayer is followed by the praying of the rosary proper.

In saying the rosary, we call to mind one at a time each of the mysteries as a focus of reflection. The series of prayers for each mystery begins with the recitation of the Our Father, followed by ten Hail Marys, ending with the Glory Be. This series is referred to as a *decade* because of the ten Hail Marys. After completion of the first decade, another mystery is called to mind, and the process of prayer continues.

The rosary focuses on key aspects of the Christian faith, especially as seen in the twenty mysteries. The joyful mysteries are the Annunciation, the Visitation, the Nativity, the Presentation of the Child Jesus, and the Finding of the Child Jesus in the Temple. The luminous mysteries are Christ's Baptism, the Wedding at Cana, the Proclamation of the Kingdom, the Transfiguration, and the Institution of the Eucharist. The sorrowful mysteries consist of Christ's Agony in the Garden, the Scourging, the Crowning of Thorns, the Carrying of the Cross, and the Crucifixion. Finally, the Glorious mysteries are the Resurrection, the Ascension, the Descent of the Holy Spirit, the Assumption of Mary, and the Coronation of Mary.

These meditations have been called a short course in theology because of the wealth of truth and inspiration they contain. Through meditating on these mysteries we are led to prayers of adoration, contrition, thanksgiving, and petition. It is also an opportunity for the Holy Spirit to work in our hearts and minds as we pray to bring understanding and formation.

Prayer is a communication between God and us. As we pray, not only are we turning our hearts, minds, and spirits to God, but God is also communicating his life to us. The length of time required to recite each decade gives us more opportunity for reflection and for this intimate communication with God.

Since a group can recite the rosary together, this form of prayer also has a communal aspect. In fact, in a sense the rosary can really never be prayed alone, because it is a joining with the Blessed Mother in prayer. Mary is always in an attitude of prayer before God in heaven. The rosary, through the regular recitation of the Hail Mary, is a joining with Mary in her prayer and asking her assistance.

Finally, the rosary can be a wonderful prayer of intercession. It can be prayed for a particular intention such as world peace or the needs of a family member. For this reason, many Catholics pray the rosary daily as part of their established plan of prayer. It is a versatile form of prayer that can have new meaning each time it is prayed.

History

Where and when the rosary began is unknown. The use of beads as an aid in prayer has a long history both in the Catholic Church and in other religions. The chain of beads establishes a framework for prayer. It sets a pace for the prayer, and the repetition provides a background for meditation.

Even though the beginnings of the rosary are unknown, it is undeniable that the rosary's popularity grew significantly through the preaching of St. Dominic, who died in 1221. Dominic encouraged the rosary as a remedy to heresy. The meditation on the mysteries developed a foundation of the truths of the faith. This saint also saw the prayer as an antidote to sin. As Dominic and his followers preached throughout Europe, they encouraged the rosary as a regular form of prayer for the laity.

Many popes have also encouraged this devotion. One notable

example comes from the reign of Pope Pius V (1566–1572). At that time the Turkish Moslems were actively seeking to conquer Christian Europe. They were having significant success in their endeavors, and Europe was in real peril.

Pope Pius asked all the faithful to pray and ask for Mary's intercession that the Turkish threat would be halted. In particular, Pius encouraged the praying of the rosary. In the famous Battle of Lepanto on October 7, 1571, the Christian forces defeated the Turkish fleet and effectively ended the threat of conquest by the Moslems. To acknowledge the effectiveness of praying the rosary and to thank the Blessed Mother for her intercession, Pius established the Feast of the Holy Rosary to be celebrated each October.

The word *rosary* comes from the Latin *rosarius*, which means "garland" or "bouquet of flowers." It is an apt word for a bouquet of prayers offered to God. The word *bead* is an Old English term that originally meant "a prayer."

Use

As with any sacramental, prayer, or devotion, the rosary can be a tremendous aid in drawing closer to God. However, it can also be misused. The structure and flow of the prayer of the rosary is meant to aid the individual in meditation. The rhythm of the prayer can quiet the spirit and make a person more receptive to hearing God and thus being formed spiritually.

For some, however, the rosary can become a merely mechanical action, something to be rushed through as a duty. It is important to recall that the grace of any sacramental is dependent upon the attitude of the person using it. Thus devout and thoughtful use of the rosary is a prerequisite to enjoying the grace of the devotion.

Pilgrimage

Life is a journey. The Catholic sees that journey as something purposeful. We have a destination; we are bound for heaven, eternal life, and happiness with God. The journey is a time of grace, a time to grow in love of God and service to his people. Saints are born and mature in that journey of life.

Someone who makes a journey for a spiritual purpose is called a *pilgrim*, and the journey is known as a *pilgrimage*. Pilgrims make such journeys for various reasons:

To venerate a holy place, a sacred object, or a relic.
To offer thanksgiving for God's blessing.
As a sign of repentance.
To imitate Jesus or one of the saints.

Traditionally, the pilgrimage has been undertaken as a time of prayer and turning to God. God's grace is sought not only for the specific journey to a particular place, but also for the journey of life that will culminate in eternal life with God.

Destinations

Two biblical accounts of journeys provide the precedents for later pilgrimages. The first is the Exodus of the Israelites from Egypt to Zion, the Promised Land.

The people of the Exodus prepared for the journey by offering sacrifice to God and seeking his protection. They undertook the journey carrying few provisions and trusting in him to meet their needs. During the time of journey, God worked with the Israelites to form them as individuals and as a people. They eventually came to the Promised Land, where God established them.

The other journey that provides the prototype of all other pilgrimages is the journey of Jesus to Jerusalem and ultimately to his crucifixion. In many ways the entire gospel describes that journey.

After Christianity spread to Europe, many people developed a desire to see the lands where Jesus had lived and died. Therefore, Jerusalem and the Holy Land became the first popular sites for pilgrims who desired to walk in the footsteps of Jesus.

A second popular destination for pilgrims was Rome, the city where Sts. Peter and Paul had been martyred. These pilgrimages to Rome increased during years that were declared "Holy Years" or "Jubilee Years." The first officially organized celebration of a Holy Year was called by Pope Boniface in the year 1300. However, before this time there had been a tradition of celebrating every century and half-century mark as a special time of prayer and celebration. On these occasions pilgrimages to Rome increased significantly.

Pilgrims flocked to many other destinations throughout the Christian world, but especially in the West, where this tradition was particularly strong. Pilgrimage destinations included shrines dedicated to the Blessed Mother, burial locations of saints, and places where martyrs had given witness to the faith with their very lives.

Garb

During the Middle Ages pilgrimages were at their peak. Pilgrims were expected to pray specific prayers as part of the devotion and to carry distinctive standards. Their garb identified them as people on a spiritual journey.

The pilgrim's clothes were to be simple. They were to travel with minimal possessions and rely on God and the charity of others to help meet the needs of the journey. They often wore a distinctive hood on their cloak, and they carried a staff.

They also wore a badge that hung around their neck or was pinned to their clothing. These badges might include some symbol of their destination or might display a picture of the Blessed Mother or of a saint. Almost always the badge included the cross in its design.

Blessings and Prayers

Before embarking on the pilgrimage, those making the journey would ask for the prayers and blessings of the Church. The staff and garb of the pilgrim were blessed. Prayers were offered that the person on the journey would receive God's protection and that the fruit of the journey would be an increase in grace and holiness of life.

Here is an example of a blessing prayed over the badge and staff:

> We humbly call upon you [Lord], that you would be pleased to bless this scrip [badge] and this staff that whosoever for love of your name shall desire to wear the same at his side or hang it at his neck or to bear it in his hands and so on his pilgrimage to seek the aid of the saints with the accompaniment of humble prayer ... may be found ready to attain the joys of the everlasting vision of you, O Savior of the world.

Crusaders

The Crusades were an outgrowth of the pilgrimage spirit. Muslims had conquered and controlled the key sites of pilgrimage in the Holy Land. At times the local Muslim governments were accommodating of Christian pilgrims. At other times it was impossible for Christians to make the journey safely to Jerusalem, Bethlehem, Nazareth, and other locations in the Holy Land.

Many Christians also felt that the land where Jesus had lived and died should be in the hands of Christians. So when the Crusades were proclaimed, a spirit of pilgrimage was encouraged. Church leaders urged the crusaders to see their efforts in the context of a holy journey.

For this reason, the crusaders adopted the traditional pilgrims' practice of wearing distinctive garb. They "took up the cross" by wearing that insignia. They were called to prepare for the Crusades with times of prayer, fasting, and repentance. Even though many crusaders were guilty of abuses, many others sought to live the true pilgrim spirit.

Modern Pilgrims
Although much of the formal structure that surrounded pilgrimages in the past has disappeared, pilgrimages are still practiced regularly by Christians. The Holy Land and Rome continue to be the primary destinations for modern pilgrims. Others go to shrines such as Lourdes or Fatima. World Youth Day, which is now being celebrated every three years, is a type of pilgrimage in which young people from around the world journey to one place to join in prayer and listen to the pope or his representative.

These modern pilgrims are still encouraged to undertake their journeys with a spirit of prayer, repentance, and trust in God. Often when a group makes a pilgrimage, the community will send them forth with a special prayer service that includes a blessing by a priest. Usually this takes place within the context of a Mass offered for the pilgrims. The prayers focus on asking God to use the trip as a time of spiritual growth for those embarking on the journey.

In addition to longer journeys, individuals can participate in the spirit of a pilgrimage by making short trips with a prayerful intent of drawing closer to God. In these cases, the pilgrimage could involve a car ride across town to visit a local church or shrine. The pilgrim might say the joyful mysteries of the rosary on the way to the destination. The sorrowful mysteries could be said before the tabernacle in the church or the shrine, and the glorious mysteries said on the trip back home. This type of pilgrimage can make an excellent family devotion.

A local pilgrimage can be made at any time, but certain times are particularly appropriate for such a journey. For example, Lent is a good time for a pilgrimage. This season calls us to a spiritual journey of repentance and drawing closer to God. A pilgrimage could be made, for example, to an outdoor setting for the stations of the cross.

Christmas is another good time for a short pilgrimage. Here the journey is made in imitation of the Magi who traveled to see the newborn king in Bethlehem. A personal pilgrimage of this sort could involve a trip to a special crèche.

The key concern here is not so much when the pilgrimage is made, nor even the destination. Instead, the attitude of the pilgrim is what makes the journey effective.

Genuflection

When you are introduced to someone, you know exactly how to handle the meeting. You extend your hand for a handshake. It expresses your intention to meet this new acquaintance as an equal.

Your handshake conveys an attitude of openness, welcome, and trust. Yet it also maintains a certain distance. In essence, you keep the person at arm's length. The handshake is an appropriate physical expression for the situation—friendly, but not too intimate.

All societies develop physical expressions that appropriately convey a relationship between individuals. In another culture, the handshake may be replaced by a bow or other gesture. The action may vary, but the basic principle remains the same. The action expresses the quality of the relationship.

Various physical expressions are appropriate in differing situations. When you meet a friend, you may exchange a hug or give a kiss on the cheek, which reflects a certain degree of closeness with that friend. If you had the opportunity to enter into the presence of a king or queen, a curtsy or bow would be an appropriate initial reaction instead.

What then should be the appropriate physical gesture when we come into the presence of God? The Scriptures are replete with examples.

Moses removed his shoes and hid his face (see Ex 3:5-6) when God appeared in the burning bush. Whenever God's presence appeared in the form of a cloud, the Israelites would stand at attention at the entrance of their tents (see Ex 33:10). Falling on one's face seems to be the most common scriptural response to meeting God (see Rv 1:17; Acts 9:4; and similar passages).

"Bending the knee" is also identified in the Scripture as an appropriate response to God. Through Isaiah the prophet, God directs that "every knee shall bow" to him (see Is 45:23). In the Letter to the Philippians, Paul echoes this language when he states that "at the name of Jesus every knee should bow" (Phil 2:10).

Genuflection is this bowing or bending of the knee. It is a physical expression of our relationship to God. Note that a genuflection is not made to an object such as a cross, altar, or even the tabernacle. The Catholic genuflects to God.

Now, it is unlikely that today God would appear in a burning bush or in a cloud. However, the eternal Son of God, Jesus, is present whole and entire under the appearances of wine and bread after the priest speaks the words of the consecration at Mass. Most Catholic churches keep the Eucharist—Jesus truly present—in a tabernacle in the Church or in an attached chapel. So when a Catholic enters a church, he will turn toward Jesus present in the tabernacle and bend his right knee until it touches the floor. A silent prayer or the making of the sign of the cross may accompany the action.

Genuflecting, then, is a sign of reverence and an acknowledgement of the position of the creature before the Creator and of the sinner before the Savior. Worship and adoration are the correct response to God. Genuflection expresses and affirms that position and response.

Given its meaning, genuflection should be done in a reverential manner. "This act requires that it be performed in a recollected way. In order that the heart may bow before God in profound reverence, the genuflection must be neither hurried nor careless."[3]

A Unique Expression

Genuflection is not a universal custom. In the Eastern Church a profound bow toward Christ in the Eucharist is the normal action.

Historically, people would genuflect to a monarch, a bishop, or the pope as an acknowledgement of the individual's position of authority. In our time this custom has almost disappeared. This development allows a genuflection to be a unique expression of our relationship to God.

Liturgical Vestments

While it is not really true that the "clothes make the man," as the old saying goes, a person's apparel can nevertheless have an impact. Special clothing or a uniform can signify authority, power, distinction, or an official designation. So police, firefighters, theater ushers, and the Queen of England all wear garments that distinguish their position and office.

In a similar way, all Catholic clergy, from the local deacon to the pope, wear distinctive garments when involved in liturgical functions. These garments collectively are known as *vestments*. The word has its origin in a Latin word which means "to clothe."

In the Old Testament, Jewish priests wore certain distinctive apparel while performing the temple sacrifices. But the garb of the Catholic priest probably did not evolve directly from the customary dress of the Jewish priest. In the time before Emperor Constantine (the fourth century), the priestly dress probably did not differ from the standard dress of the Greco-Roman world. As styles changed, however, the clergy continued to wear the original Greco-Roman dress when involved in liturgical functions.

Stole

The earliest item to be worn specifically to designate a deacon, priest, or bishop was probably the *stole*. The stole is a long strip of cloth that the priest and bishop wear around the neck, with both ends hanging over the chest. A deacon wears the stole over the left shoulder, across the chest, with the two ends of the strip fastened on the right side.

The stole is a symbol of the office of the ordained clergy and is worn by the minister when administering the sacraments or when preaching. (Often it is not visible because it is worn under the *chasuble* or the *dalmatic*—see below.) The color of the stole matches the color of the outer liturgical garment. In the past, a crucifix was embroidered on each end and in the middle of the stole. However, this practice is not as prevalent today.

Alb

When a priest vests for Mass, the garment he puts on first is the *alb*. This is a floor-length white gown that covers his other clothing. It takes its name from the Latin word for "white." The present-day alb has its origin in a Roman garment, the *tunica talaris*—a tunic that reached to the ankles.

This vestment, while always white, may be augmented by lace or embroidery. Traditionally it was fastened at the waist by a rope called a *cincture*. The cincture in many instances has now been replaced by more modern methods of fastening such as Velcro.

Chasuble and Dalmatic

The outer liturgical garment worn at Mass also has a Greco-Roman origin. It is based upon an ancient Roman outer garment. The Latin word *casula,* from which we get *chasuble,* means "little house"—an appropriate name for a garment that covers the wearer.

The chasuble, a free-flowing garment with a hole for the head, is worn by the priest and bishop. The *dalmatic,* worn by the deacon, is based upon a particular type of ancient outer garment that originated in the area of Dalmatia in Asia Minor. The design of these vestments varies widely from the very ornate to quite simple. Their color reflects the liturgical season or feast.

Cope

The *cope* is a specialized liturgical garment. It resembles a cloak and is worn at the Benediction of the Blessed Sacrament, in various processions, and in some solemn liturgies. The cope is worn over the shoulders and fastened at the chest; it extends to the floor.

Humeral Veil

A cloth of rectangular shape, the *humeral veil* is used by a priest to hold the vessel containing the Blessed Sacrament at Benediction or during a procession, and also by an acolyte to hold the bishop's mitre at solemn liturgies. When used to hold the *monstrance* or *ciborium* (vessels for holding the Blessed Sacrament), this "extra" garment emphasizes the importance of the Eucharist and the reverence that is due to the Body and Blood of Christ.

Liturgical Colors

The color of the vestments varies during the course of the Church's liturgical year. There are some variations between the Eastern rite and Latin rite churches.

In the West, white is the color for feasts of our Lord, except his Passion. White is also used on Marian feasts, celebrations of saints who are not martyrs, feasts of angels, and during Christmas and Easter. Red is worn on the feasts of martyrs, on Pentecost, and on Palm Sunday and Good Friday.

Purple is the color for Advent and Lent. Green is worn during "ordinary" time in the liturgical year. Two other colors are permitted for liturgical use. Rose-colored vestments can be worn on *Laetare* Sunday (the fourth Sunday) in Lent and *Gaudate* Sunday (the third Sunday) in Advent. Black is permissible for funeral Masses, although white is more commonly used.

Blessing

Vestments and other objects used in liturgical rites usually are blessed prior to use. The blessing dedicates the article for a sacred use. Once blessed, the object is to be used only for the intended purpose. So you wouldn't see a priest wearing a chasuble at the local high school football game or using an altar cloth for the table at a Wednesday night dinner.

The blessing for liturgical vestments indicates their special nature and asks God that their use would bring a spirit of reverence and grace: "May your ministers who use these vestments, prepared for the celebration of the liturgy and set apart by your blessing, wear them with reverence and honor them by the holiness of their lives."[4]

The Altar and Items Used at Mass

The Mass is both a meal and a sacrifice. The altar in every church reflects both aspects. An altar was used in the Hebrew temple sacrifices. As a matter of fact, the root of the Hebrew word for *altar* means "to slaughter" or "to sacrifice." On the altars in Catholic Churches, the sacrifice of Jesus on the cross is made present again at each Mass in an "unbloody" manner.

At the same time, the Eucharist is also a meal in which the faithful receive spiritual food, the very Body and Blood of Christ. In the early Church the Mass was celebrated in the homes of Christians. Here the table of the house was used for the Eucharistic meal. As the Christian community grew in numbers and churches were built, the altars continued to be movable wooden structures that resembled tables.

Around the fourth century altars took on more significance and began to be made of more permanent materials such as metal or stone. They began to resemble more the altar of the Jewish temple than a table in a home.

With altars fixed in one place, another feature was added. Relics were placed into a recess in the top of the altar. Early in the history of the Church, Mass had been celebrated at the graves of martyrs to remember and venerate them. Early churches had been built over the burial sites of martyrs. Placing relics in the altar was thus an outgrowth of this ancient practice. Today this practice is no longer required but is encouraged, especially in altars that are permanently fixed within a church.

There was a time when a single church could have several altars. Now the instructions on the liturgy specify that there should only be one altar in the Church as a symbol of the one Christ who is the Head and Center of one community. If the church contains chapels, however, each chapel may contain an altar.

If an altar is permanently affixed to a particular location in the Church, it is customary and recommended that the bishop perform the blessing of the altar. When the altar is movable and of a more temporary nature, the blessing can be performed by a priest.

Altar Cloths

Because the Eucharist is offered on the altar, the altar has always been treated with respect as a symbol of Christ present to his people. From the time of the early Church a cloth was placed over the altar as a sign of this respect. Eventually the tradition grew of covering the altar with two or three cloths.

The cloth closest to the altar was made of a more costly material. The upper cloth was traditionally made of linen or hemp because of the durability of the fabric. Today, one cloth is commonly used, and the material may vary. Altar cloths have always been white.

Corporal

The *corporal* is a small linen cloth used during Mass and during other liturgies that involve the Eucharist. The word is derived from the Latin *corpus*, "body." Thus on this cloth is placed the Body of Christ. After use it is folded into nine squares with care in case any particles of the Blessed Sacrament have fallen onto the cloth.

Paten, Ciborium, and Chalice

A vessel that resembles a dish, the *paten* holds the bread that becomes the Body of Christ during the Mass and is used both before and after the consecration. The *ciborium* (from Latin *cibus*, "food") is a larger vessel that holds a larger amount of bread, which, after becoming Christ's Body in the consecration, will be offered to the faithful for Communion.

The *chalice* holds the wine that will become the Blood of Christ at the consecration. "Chalice" is derived from a Latin word that means "cup" or "goblet."

Traditionally these vessels have been made of precious metals such as silver, gold, or brass. However, the present requirement is only that the material must be solid and not porous, and of a material not easily broken.

Because they will hold the Body and Blood of Christ, the paten, ciborium, and chalice receive a special blessing. The celebrant prays in this blessing that the vessels "may be sanctified, for in them the Body and Blood of Christ will be offered, consecrated, and received." After the blessing the liturgical items are permanently set aside for the celebration of the Eucharist. As sacred vessels they cannot be used for anything other than the liturgy.

Purificator

The *purificator* is the cloth used to cleanse the vessels (chalice, ciborium, and paten) that have contained the consecrated Elements. It is used to catch any drops of the sacred Blood when Communion is distributed under both species. These cloths are handled with care and laundered with special care because of their use with the Eucharist.

Other Items on the Altar

A crucifix and candles are often set on or near the altar. Care must be taken that these items not obstruct the view of the congregation. The book that the priest or bishop uses at the altar is called the *Sacramentary.*

A small, stiff, cloth-covered board is sometimes set on top of the chalice. This *pall* is to keep the precious Blood from contamination.

A cloth veil of the same color as the liturgical vestments is sometimes placed over the chalice when it is carried to and from the altar.

Devotional Medals

People often make statements or place advertisements through what they wear or place on their cars. Some T-shirts inform everyone who cares to look that the wearer enjoys the music of some rock group, likes a particular beer, or is concerned about some environmental issue. Car bumper stickers make statements about political candidates or offer opinions about other drivers.

Religious medals have a much longer history than T-shirts and bumper stickers, but they too make a statement on behalf of the wearer. Medals can be made of wood, metal, plastic, or other material. Usually they are worn around the neck, but they may also be pinned to clothing.

Such medals are intended to encourage religious devotion and prayer. Many depict our Lord, the Blessed Mother, or some saint. The wearer asks the protection and help of the person whose image is displayed.

Often the wearing of a medal demonstrates a particular devotion. For example, a husband and father may wear a medal that portrays St. Joseph. In doing so, he is asking St. Joseph to help him and intercede so that he may follow in the footsteps of the husband of Mary and the foster father of Jesus.

Sometimes the medal may demonstrate affiliation with a particular devotion or prayer. The Miraculous Medal and the Divine Mercy are examples of this type. Medals may also be a sign of consecration, such as consecration to the Sacred Heart of Jesus.

Medals can be a witness to others of the wearer's faith. However, their primary function is to increase the devotion of those who wear them. Every time the wearers feel that medal against their chest, or look at it upon their lapel, it provides an opportunity to offer a prayer. The medal also serves as a constant reminder to them of the responsibilities of being a Catholic who seeks to live a godly life.

Medals can be blessed by a priest or deacon. In this way they qualify as sacramentals and are joined to the many graces and prayers of the Church. In the blessing of medals the priest or deacon may say to the one who has brought the item to be blessed: "The symbols of religious devotion that you have brought to be blessed express your faith in various ways: they serve to bring to mind our Lord's great love for us or to increase our confidence in the power of Mary and the saints to help us."[5]

Medals are not magic amulets. They are symbols of faith and devotion. Their value lies in the relationship between those who wear them and God, Mary, and the saints. The medal is an instrument to help the believer maintain and foster that relationship.

Scapular

A scapular represents a person's association with a religious order or a particular mode of spirituality that is practiced or promulgated by an order. The word scapular derives from the Latin word for "shoulder." Originally it was a garment placed over the head and hung on the shoulders. Half of the garment hung in front and half on the back. Typically it hung to the floor.

Today various orders continue to wear this type of scapular. The scapular is bestowed upon the person entering the religious order and thereby becomes a sign of membership. It is also a sign that the monk, friar, nun, or sister has accepted the rules and spirituality of that particular religious order, whether it is a particular form of prayer or a certain type of work (such as commitment to work with the sick or poor).

Lay people are unable to participate fully in the life of a given religious order because of their state in life and other responsibilities. However, some lay people wish to identify with the prayer life or ministry of an order and seek to live a life that is compatible with that of the religious. These Christians developed the custom of being invested with a scapular of a smaller variety as a sign of their association with the order.

These small scapulars are little patches of cloth that contain artwork particular to the religious order. Two long cords connect these bits of cloth. In the same fashion as the full scapular, these are placed over the head and rest on the shoulders with part hanging in front and part on the back.

Investiture

The scapular is normally bestowed during a communal celebration. A priest of the religious order will conduct the investiture with specific prayers varying according to the religious institution. By taking on the scapular, the recipients join spiritually to the life of the religious congregation and agree to live by certain norms that have been prescribed. They also pledge to support the work of the religious group and its ministry by prayer and good works.

There are a variety of scapulars; each is affiliated with a different religious institution. The most popular is the "Brown Scapular" of the Carmelite order. It is probably the oldest scapular and was the prototype for others. According to tradition, the Blessed Mother appeared to St. Simon Stock in 1251. Mary directed Simon to wear the brown scapular as a sign of dedication to her as a protector of the order. The scapular then served both as a badge of devotion to Mary and as a sign of her protection.

Other religious orders, such as the Trinitarians, the Servite Order, the Confraternity of the Precious Blood, the Passionist Fathers, the Sisters of Charity of St. Vincent de Paul, and others have unique scapulars that can be conferred upon laity who wish to follow the particular rule of their congregation.

The Cross and the Crucifix

Businessmen and women know the value of developing a logo that identifies their company in the eyes of the public. Christians, too, have a logo; it is the cross, the symbol with which they have long been associated.

In the ancient Roman Empire, of course, the cross was the instrument of torture and death reserved for the worst of criminals. It was a most ignominious way to die, so Roman citizens were spared this form of death. Because of the calculated brutality of this method of execution, it was generally reserved for outsiders.

This association made the cross an unlikely "logo" for any group. Nonetheless, it became the symbol that most readily identified the Christian. In fact, early Christians were called "cross worshipers" in derision by the surrounding pagan society.

Christians chose the cross as the most visible sign of their faith because it was through this instrument of death that Jesus had brought life to them. St. Paul summarized the belief of Christians when he wrote: "The cross is folly to those who are perishing, but to us who are being saved it is the power of God" (1 Cor 1:18).

As the Christian Church came under persecution, however, the cross easily identified followers of Christ as targets for persecution. So Christians found ways to maintain the symbol of the cross while also disguising it to unbelievers. For example, the Greek letter *Tau* (T) was used and known by Christians to represent the cross.

With the conversion of the Roman Emperor Constantine, Christianity found new acceptance in the Roman world. The cross, as a visible emblem, returned to regular usage. The use of the cross as the most prominent Christian symbol was further enhanced in A.D. 326 when St. Helena, mother of the Emperor Constantine, became instrumental in the discovery of the cross of Christ in Jerusalem.

Public veneration of the true cross of Christ and of crosses of similar design became common. Christians began to wear a small cross around their neck as a symbol of their faith. Portions of the true cross were distributed throughout the Christian world and were displayed in cross-shaped reliquaries[6] for public veneration. Even the design of church architecture reflected devotion to the cross as church buildings took the form of a cross.

This devotion to the cross prompted a caution from the great St. Ambrose: "Let us adore Christ, our King, who hung upon the wood,

130 / Catholic Customs

and not the wood." The cross was a powerful symbol and point of reference for Christian belief. But it was in danger of being an end in itself rather than a means to draw closer to God and to worship him alone.

In the eighth century, realistic depictions of Christ on the cross began to appear. By the eleventh century, the crucifix was common in the Western Church. As with other art forms, the Church in the West preferred three-dimensional depictions. In the East the figure of Christ crucified generally appeared in the two-dimensional icon instead.

The crucifix eventually became a regular feature on the altar. There, it provided a visual connection between the unbloody Sacrifice of the altar and the Crucifixion.

At the time of the Protestant Reformation, many Catholic customs were challenged. Some of the reformed traditions such as Lutheranism and Anglicanism kept the crucifix as an object to prompt devotion, while other reformers rejected the crucifix along with other liturgical art. Nevertheless, the display of the cross or crucifix continues to have three values for the Christian: instruction, devotion, and witness.

As with other art of a Christian theme, the cross or crucifix is intended to instruct. The truths of the redemptive life and death of Christ are reinforced by this visual image. At the same time, for many believers the crucifix provides a point of focus while in prayer—a great help in overcoming distractions and turning the mind and heart to God.

Thus many Catholics pray with a crucifix before them. It is not that the crucifix is the object of prayer. Rather it is a means to draw closer to Christ and to consider his love—an encouragement to devotion.

For the early Christians the cross was a sign that identified a person as a follower of Jesus. It was readily identified as such in the secular society. Today the cross sometimes serves the same purpose.

For some people, of course, a cross is only another piece of jewelry and nothing more. Yet for many Christians the wearing of a cross or crucifix serves as a testimony. It makes the statement: "I wear this because I am a follower of Jesus." In this way it provides an opportunity to give witness and, in some small way, to follow the direction of Christ to "proclaim the good news."

Finally, for many Catholics, wearing a cross or crucifix also serves as a kind of witness to themselves—a reminder to live a Christian life and to turn to God in prayer during the day.

Candles

Something about the flickering flame of a candle captures attention and inspires awe. Flame, light, and candles have been used in the rituals of many religions. Not surprisingly, the Catholic Church has incorporated the use of candles into its own liturgy.

In the Gospel of John, Jesus calls himself "the light of the world" (Jn 8:12). The Paschal candle is a symbol of the eternal light that came into the world through Jesus. As we noted earlier, the Paschal candle is blessed and first lit at Easter. Small candles held by the congregation are then lit from it.

The symbolism is clear. Each Christian is to take the light of Christ and shine it to the rest of the world—bringing light into the darkness. That is why the Paschal candle is also utilized in the baptism ceremony at the Easter Vigil and at other baptisms throughout the year.

Candles, and their predecessors, oil lamps, have had other uses as well in the Christian tradition. From the earliest times of the Church, lamps were lit at the tombs of the dead, especially at the graves of the martyrs. This custom honored the faithful departed and, probably, served also as a reminder to pray.

Today many churches give people the opportunity to light candles before a shrine. The shrine may be a depiction of our Lord, the Blessed Mother, or another saint. The meaning of this custom continues from the earlier practice of placing lamps at the graves of the martyrs.

First, it is one way to honor our Lord or the saint. Second, it is a sign of prayer. Those who light a candle at a shrine of the Blessed Mother, for example, usually ask Mary to intercede for a special intention. The candle, which remains lit, serves as a sign that prayer continues. Mary continually prays for the intentions that are brought to her. The person lighting the candle should also persevere in prayer. Meanwhile, the many lights before the shrine will encourage and inspire others to prayer.

Candles have also been used to add splendor to liturgical celebrations. From about the eleventh century candles have been required at the altar during Mass. In the past the number of candles varied depending on the solemnity of the liturgy. Under present guidelines, two candles are used at the celebration of the Mass. They may be placed on the altar or at a place near the altar.

Originally, candles used in the liturgy were to be made only of beeswax. This was to symbolize the "pure flesh of Christ received from the Virgin Mary."[7]

A candle or other light is kept burning near every tabernacle in Catholic Churches wherever the Eucharist is reserved. The small flame is a reminder to all who visit that the Light of the world is truly present in that tabernacle, awaiting those who would come to visit, pray, and reflect.

Incense

Incense is another liturgical element not unique to the Catholic Church. It has been used since early times to honor monarchs and pagan gods. However, the Church has used incense to enhance worship within her own liturgies, continuing the ancient Jewish custom.

Incense is granulated aromatic resin. Typically it is sprinkled on burning coals housed in a *censer* (also called a *thurible*). The fragrant smoke rises from the censer as a sign of honor, worship, and prayer.

The use of incense is more common in the Eastern Church than in the Western Church. In Eastern rites incense is used at almost every liturgy to display respect for the Word of God in the Book of the Gospels and to show reverence for the altar.

In the Latin rite incense is usually reserved for particularly solemn occasions, although it may be used at any Mass. Upon entering the Church in procession the celebrant may incense the altar. The Book of the Gospel may be honored with incense prior to the reading of the Gospel.

The gifts, the congregation, and the celebrant may also be incensed during the offertory. Here the symbolism is one of purification. Incense is also used during Eucharistic processions to honor Christ in the Eucharist and add solemnity to the occasion.

Another effect of incense is to prompt prayer. The fragrant smoke rising from the altar is intended as a sign of the prayers of the community rising to God. The book of Revelation is instructive in this regard: "The smoke of the incense rose with the prayers of the saints from the hand of the angel before God" (Rv 8:4).

Incense is also prescribed for use during the funeral liturgy. The body of the deceased was the temple of the Holy Spirit in life, so in death the body is honored with incense.

The Catholic Cemetery

The Code of Canon Law of the Catholic Church defines two places as "sacred." One is the Catholic church, and the other is the Catholic cemetery.

The church is a sacred place because there, God has become present on the altar and remains in the tabernacle whenever the Eucharist is reserved. Even when a church is to be abandoned, there is a special ceremony to end its use as a sacred place. God has visited and dwelt in that building. Therefore, it is to be treated with respect.

The Catholic cemetery is considered sacred for a similar reason. Men and women are made in the image of God and contain the "breath of life" (see Gn 2:7) that comes only from God. However, God has done more than merely create men and women. In Baptism the Holy Spirit actually enters the life of the baptized. God takes up residence within that individual.

Therefore, the body is to be respected. Even in death, when the soul has left the body, the body is yet to be respected, because God has dwelt there. Thus the Church has always encouraged respectful burial and has maintained cemeteries for the burial of the faithful.

In addition, the Church has always professed belief in "the resurrection of the dead."[8] At the end of time will come a final judgment, and the dead will be raised. God's kingdom will be fully realized. There will be a new heaven and a new earth. The soul of every person who has ever lived will be reunited with its body.

Men are not angels, nor are they pure spirits. In God's plan, body and soul will be reunited to live in his kingdom forever. The Catholic cemetery is a witness to that truth. In fact, Catholic cemeteries are often called places where the bodies of the faithful departed rest while they await the final resurrection.

Consecrated cemeteries can be traced back to the very beginning of the Church. The graves and tombs of the martyrs were given special veneration. The catacombs in Rome bear witness to the care given to the burial of the dead and to the preservation of these places of burial.

Whenever a new Catholic cemetery is opened, it receives a special blessing. The normal minister of this blessing is the bishop of the diocese where the cemetery is located. Whenever a Catholic is buried in a non-Catholic cemetery, an extra prayer is added at the committal service to bless that particular burial space. This prayer is not necessary in the Catholic cemetery because the entire cemetery has been specifically blessed for burial of the faithful departed.

Cremation

In the past, some opponents of the Catholic Church practiced cremation as a denial of the Catholic belief in the resurrection of the body at the time of the final judgment. Of course, the practice of cremation in defiance of Church teaching was actually a misunderstanding of the teaching of the Church. God does not need the physical remains of the individual that are placed in the grave to created a glorified body for an individual (see Mt 3:9).

Nonetheless, because cremation was practiced as a denial of Church teaching, it was banned for the Catholic. Today, however, because cremation is sometimes practiced for cultural or financial reasons, it is permitted. (The rule was changed when Canon Law was revised in 1983.) However, the cremated remains of the deceased are still to be treated with respect, and burial is strongly encouraged.

In the cemetery or the church, at home or on pilgrimage, in the bright colors of vestments or the dark cloud of incense, we encounter the power of sacramentals and other signs. In countless ways, these sacred visual images provide us opportunities to cooperate with the working of God's grace.

FOUR

Patterns of Prayer

Prayer is communication with God that seeks union with him. It is the opportunity for the creature to relate to the Creator, the saved reaching out to the Savior. It is need looking to the Answer with hope and trust. And this is possible only because God permits it and enables it, since it is the Holy Spirit that prompts and guides prayer (see Rom 8:26).

Prayer is foundational in the Christian life. Since the intended destiny for all men and women is eternal life with God, prayer is a vehicle for beginning and continuing that relationship with him while on earth. Therefore, prayer is an eternal reality. The saints in heaven and the souls undergoing purification in purgatory pray. Only the damned do not pray, because they have rejected God's invitation to a relationship of love with him.

To Whom Do We Pray?

Prayer is directed to God. It can be addressed to a specific person of the Holy Trinity: Father, Son, or Holy Spirit. Liturgical prayer usually includes all three Persons of the Trinity in its formulae. The prayer may initially address God the Father but then end with a phrase that includes the other persons of the Trinity: "through our Lord Jesus Christ, your Son, who lives and reigns in unity with the Holy Spirit." If the prayer is initially addressed to the Son, it may end this way:

"Who lives and reigns with God the Father in union with the Holy Spirit."

The aim and goal of prayer is always a relationship with God. However, prayer can take an intermediate course through the intercession of the saints and angels. These dwellers in heaven constantly stand before the throne of God and can offer prayer on our behalf.

Why Pray?

Why do we speak to our parents or spouse? We do so because it is a vital means of communication and growth in relationship and intimacy.

It is the same with God. He has ordained prayer as a method for reaching out to him, knowing him, and growing in intimacy with him. Prayer is effective, as affirmed in the Scripture. "Ask, and it will be given you; seek, and you will find" (Mt 7:7). "Whatever you ask in prayer, believe that you receive it, and you will" (Mk 11:24).

God gives to his children, and he does not give a scorpion when we have asked for an egg (see Lk 11:12). This does not mean that we will get exactly what we request. God is a merciful Father who wants the best for his children. He also sees from an eternal perspective and knows what will be a true blessing for us. Therefore, for our benefit the answer to the prayer may differ from the request. Nonetheless, the prayer is heard and the answer is given—an answer that will bless and benefit us.

Another important reason to pray is that it changes the person who prays. Prayer is an encounter with God, who is the Creator and the One who gives life. When Moses spoke with God, he returned as a changed man. Even his features were changed (see Ex 34:29-35). That experience is typical of all prayer. A sincere encounter with God can change and form us, making us more Christlike.

How to Pray

Many books have been written on techniques of prayer. In the material that follows we will focus on some of the customary and traditional prayers in the Catholic tradition. Techniques, forms, and methods can be helpful because they provide a structure. However, prayer is ultimately a person turning heart and mind to God with the desire to relate to him.

Does a child need a technique to relate to her mother? All the child needs to do is reach out her arms. Prayer is the same. The soul reaches out to God.

While structure is helpful, right attitude and perspective in prayer are of utmost importance. The subject matter of prayer should be worthy of God and for the good of the one who prays. This is not to imply that God is not concerned about every aspect of our lives. He is. However, a good way to start any prayer of intercession is to consider whether the request is worthy of God and for the good. For example, praying that my neighbor would have a car wreck because I dislike him is unlikely to be worthy subject matter for prayer!

In addition, implicit in every prayer should be the caveat "if it be your will." God wants the best for us. When we make a request of him, even a request about which we feel strongly, we should want primarily his will.

This attitude is not always easy to maintain. If the prayer is that a loved one be spared pain or death, it is difficult to add, "If it be your will." However, if this submission to the will of God is the habitual approach of the person in prayer, such an attitude is likely to continue even under difficult circumstances.

God is immeasurably greater than we are. His knowledge, power, understanding, wisdom, and love are far superior to ours. So an attitude of humility is necessary for the person who prays.

We do not demand from God, and he owes us nothing. We do ask, and we do so as a child would make a request of a loving parent. So we ask with confidence, but also with humility.

Sincerity is another important component in prayer. You may recall the familiar joke about the man who continually asks God to allow him to win the lottery and becomes frustrated when it doesn't occur. God then speaks from the clouds: "Do me a favor; buy a ticket!"

Well, not only did that prayer lack worthy subject matter; it also lacked sincerity. We need to work on those requests for which we pray. For example, if we ask God to make us less angry, we need to co-operate with his grace by trying to control our anger, repenting when we do lose our temper, and seeking the help of others. Another example would be the man who asks God's help to control lust. If the man is sincere, he will avoid situations of temptation while he also perseveres in prayer.

The last important component of prayer is attention. The Bible warns against the mindless repetition of words (see Mt 6:7). Praying is not in the words but in the turning of the mind and heart to God.

Formula prayers can be a tremendous help in prayer. However, when they are said without focus and intention, they are mere words.

Now that doesn't mean that the amount of attention in prayer cannot vary. For example, someone driving to work may have a desire to pray and so begin to say the rosary. However, the driver still must pay attention to driving and thus cannot give 100 percent attention to the meditations of the rosary. Nevertheless, this is still prayer because the intention of the one praying is to give his or her heart and mind to God in the degree possible under the circumstances.

Even so, praying when thoughts are divided and distractions abound is not the best approach. So the Church has always recommended setting specific time aside for concentrated prayer—much like making an appointment with God. During these times, God can be the sole focus. Distractions will come during any time of prayer, of course, but limiting the distractions provides a better opportunity to maintain focus.

Scripture also encourages Christians to pray at all times and to pray without ceasing (see Lk 18:1; Eph 6:18; 1 Thes 5:17). God is always present and available, so it is always possible to take a moment and turn our thoughts to God. This, too, is prayer. Such brief moments with God are not a substitute for focused prayer, but they form a valuable complement to it.

Types of Prayer

Prayer can be categorized several ways. One way is to distinguish *personal* prayer from *corporate* or *liturgical* prayer. Personal prayer is the individual relating to God. Here the person opens the heart and mind to God with expressions of thought and prayer that can be of infinite variety and cover almost any subject matter. The individual can also use formal prayers (as opposed to spontaneous prayers) as a format.

Liturgical prayer uses formula prayers in which the entire congregation can participate. Sometimes the minister prays on behalf of the entire assembly, and the assembly responds in unison. At other times, the entire congregation prays together, as in the recitation of the Our Father during Mass.

In either type of prayer the attitude of the person praying is a vital component.

Prayer can also be divided into *mental* and *vocal* prayer. All prayer has a mental component. But vocal prayer is generally spoken as well and involves some external activity.[1]

As in all prayer, vocal prayer requires an attitude of turning the heart and mind to God, but it does not involve the same degree of mental application as mental prayer. In mental prayer, the individual turns all his or her higher faculties (intellect, imagination, memory, and will) to mediate on God and his mysteries.

The Matter of Prayer

It is easier to speak of things to exclude from prayer than to speak of what to include in prayer! God is willing to hear all the concerns of his children. Yet some specific areas of concern should be regular items for prayer. These include asking for grace to persevere in the Christian life, to resist temptation, and to grow in virtue and the guidance of the Holy Spirit in daily life.

Christ gave a powerful lesson in the nature and *matter* (that is, subject matter) of prayer when he taught his disciples the Our Father. It begins with praise of God. It has a communal element. Forgiveness is sought. A desire for God's will is expressed. The person who prays asks for "daily bread." God is asked to meet the needs of the individual: mental, physical, psychological, and spiritual. Strength in resisting temptation is sought.

Prayer has traditionally included four types of matter. As creatures we owe God worship, so *adoration* is the first matter for prayer. God has given us all that we possess, so prayers of *thanksgiving* should also be a component of prayer life. All are guilty of sin when standing before a sinless God. Thus prayers of repentance and *contrition* are appropriate. Finally, *petition*—asking God to meet our needs and the needs of others—is acceptable matter for prayer.

Superstition

In April 2002 the Congregation for Divine Worship at the Vatican published the "Directory on Popular Piety and Liturgy: Principles and Guidelines." This document shows the concern of the Church that all devotions and prayer remain in keeping with the laws and norms of the universal Church. The guidelines focus on the worthiness and usefulness of specific prayers, expressions, gestures, and attitudes of popular piety that lead to growth in a person's relationship with God.

The document also cautions that all devotions should foster religious piety and not fall into superstition. There is always the danger that religious practice of any type can degenerate this way. The physical expressions of prayer and of various devotions can assist in piety, but they can also sidetrack a person into mere formalism, superstition, or the attitude that these expressions are an end in themselves.

True devotion always sees a deeper relationship with God as the goal of all practices and prayer. The various types of prayer and devotion, then, should always serve as a means to that end.

Daily Devotions

The Church has always encouraged Catholics to pray daily. It makes sense to spend time with the most important Person in your life every day. After all, this is to be an eternal relationship.

For this reason, customs of prayer have developed over time to help in weaving prayer into the fabric of the day. We are creatures of time. Time can be our enemy, but it can also be a friend. The use of daily devotions seeks to use the hours of the day to draw closer to God.

Morning Offering

A good way to begin the day is to offer it to God. The Apostleship of Prayer, a Catholic association whose members offer each day and its activities to God in union with the Holy Sacrifice of the Mass, employs this common formula prayer for a morning offering:

O Jesus, through the Immaculate Heart of Mary, I offer you all my prayers, works, joys, and sufferings of this day, for all the intentions of your Sacred Heart, in union with the Holy Sacrifice of the Mass throughout the world, in reparation for my sins, for the intentions of all our associates, and for the intentions of the Holy Father.

In essence, by offering all the thoughts and activities of the day to God, a person can make the day itself a prayer. The intention to pray is the beginning of prayer. So intending to make the activities of the day into prayers *is* making them prayers. Of course, the prayer is more effective if throughout the day we renew that morning offering and consciously turn to God at various times.

The Morning Offering is made "through the Immaculate Heart of Mary." Here Mary is asked to intercede, and the prayers of the individual are joined to those of the Mother of God.

Those who pray the Morning Offering also unite their prayers with the Mass. The Mass is the most perfect and acceptable of prayers, for in the Mass Jesus offers himself to the Father as a living sacrifice. Individuals can join themselves to Christ in that offering. Even when we cannot attend Mass on a particular day, we can join in that perpetual offering Jesus makes to his Father.

This prayer also asks that, in living a prayerful life, the temporal punishments of personal sin would be lessened. In other words, we request that grace and purification be active in our life. Yet the Morning Offering is not a self-centered prayer, since it contains intercession for others, in particular for the pope and for the intentions on his heart.

Prayer at Meals

Most people take time out periodically from the routine of the day to eat. Each meal also provides an ideal time to turn to God. Prayers at that time focus on thanksgiving and the asking of a blessing on the food and on those involved in the meal.

It also is good to remember those who are less fortunate and to pray for them at mealtimes. Many people pray at each meal for the faithful departed. As with all prayer, these table graces and blessings provide the opportunity once again to draw closer to God.

The Angelus

For generations monks have gathered at various hours of the day and night to join in communal prayer. This prayer is known as the *Liturgy of the Hours* or the *Office*. Today various religious orders of men and women continue this practice. Ordained clergy pray an abbreviated version of the Liturgy of the Hours with prayer in the morning, evening, and at night. These times of prayer are known as *Lauds*, *Vespers*, and *Compline*.

In many monasteries the custom has been to gather the monks for prayer by the ringing of the church bell. Many of the lay faithful, upon hearing the bells, would also stop their activity and take a few moments to turn to God in prayer. Over time this prayer throughout the day took on a particular form among the laity.

At 6:00 A.M., noon, and 6:00 P.M. the church bells would toll, and Catholics would stop to say the *Angelus*. The Angelus commemorates the Incarnation and birth of Jesus. It is fitting to stop a moment for this prayer during the day, because all Catholics are called to bring Christ into their daily environment, just as Mary brought Christ to the world. In recalling the Incarnation, Christians are reminded to bring Christ to those with whom they come into contact.

The Angelus is a series of four proclamations and responses. A "Hail Mary" follows the first three responses, and a final prayer ends the Angelus.

Leader: The angel of the Lord declared unto Mary.

Response: And she conceived of the Holy Spirit. (Hail Mary ...)

Leader: Behold the handmaid of the Lord.

Response: Be it done unto me according to thy word. (Hail Mary ..)

Leader: And the Word was made flesh.

Response: And dwelt among us. (Hail Mary ...)

Leader: Pray for us, O Holy Mother of God.

Response: That we may be made worthy of the promises of Christ.

Leader: Let us pray.

Response: Pour forth, we beseech thee, O Lord, thy grace into our hearts; that we, to whom the Incarnation of Christ, thy Son, was made known by the message of an angel, may by his passion and cross be brought to the glory of his resurrection. Through the same Christ our Lord. Amen.

Recalling that the Son of God became a man gives proper perspective to the day. Jesus has changed all life, including the life of each Christian, by bringing salvation. Reflecting on that fact can help bring both an attitude of thanksgiving and an eternal perspective in the midst of the business of any day.

The practice of stopping three times during the day to pray the Angelus spread in the Church over time. In 1465 Pope Calixtus III encouraged the entire Church to pray the Angelus three times a day, especially for the intention of victory over the Turks who were threatening Europe. The Franciscans also encouraged the devotion as they preached among the laity.

The Hail Mary

The Hail Mary is an integral part of the Angelus. The first two sentences of this prayer are taken directly from Scripture. The first, "Hail, Mary full of grace, the Lord is with thee, blessed art thou among women," reflects the greeting of the angel Gabriel at the Annunciation (see Lk 1:26-28). In this part of the prayer, Mary is greeted once again, this time by the one who prays, and the mystery of the Incarnation is called to mind.

The second sentence, "Blessed is the fruit of thy womb, Jesus," echoes the words of Mary's cousin, Elizabeth, when the infant John leapt in Elizabeth's womb because of the proximity of the Savior (see Lk 1:42-45). The person who prays this prayer can join in the joy of knowing that Christ is near while also paying honor to his mother.

The second part of the prayer is a petition to the Mother of God: "Holy Mary, Mother of God, pray for us sinners now and at the hour of our death." She who carried the Savior, nurtured him, and stood at the foot of the cross as he died is now at his throne in heaven and gladly will intercede for those who ask her help.

Night Prayer

The daily cycle of prayer comes to fullness as the day itself ends. The day began by our offering every thought, word, and action to God. The day comes to a close by our reviewing our success or failure in living that morning offering during that particular day.

One often-used approach to evening prayer was developed by St. Ignatius Loyola. A form of self-examination, it is not a long process. St. Ignatius arranged this time of prayer according to five points.

The first point is to thank God for the blessing of the day that is now coming to an end.

Second, we ask God for the grace to recognize the sins and failings in our life and for the grace to correct those faults.

Third, we review the day for wrongs committed in word, deed, thought, or omission. Having reviewed the day, we then ask God's forgiveness.

Finally, we renew our desire to respond to God's grace and do better the next day.

The examination during evening prayer is called a *particular examine*. In it, we review our predominant faults. These will usually only involve a few items, but they will be the areas of sin in which we are specifically striving to gain victory. We may also focus on a virtue in which we are striving to grow.

The particular examine is different from a *general examine*. The latter reviews many areas of potential sin and will use the Ten Commandments, the Beatitudes, the virtues, and other classic spiritual "lists" as points for self-examination. This is a more thorough examination of conscience and may be used in preparing for Confession.

The Catholic who regularly practices the particular examine can be compared to a businessman who regularly reviews his sales figures and then makes adjustments to reach the budgeted goal. Another analogy would be the athlete who regularly measures his success against a standard and continually works toward the goal. A regular evening examination enables the Catholic to advance in the spiritual life.

Positions of Prayer

Prayer, as we have noted, involves turning the heart and mind to God. Thus physical posture is not the most important element in prayer. Nevertheless, outward expression can manifest inner disposition and help a person to pray.

Christians' posture in prayer has varied over time and across cultures. A frequent position for prayer in the early Church was to stand with arms extended in the form of a cross. The priest now uses this posture for various liturgical prayers.

Another early posture in prayer was standing with the hands and arms raised toward heaven. The eyes often were also raised, but at times the eyes were cast down as a sign of humble submission to God.

Standing has always been a sign of respect for God in prayer.

Other prayer postures include kneeling and lying prostrate. Both of these have biblical roots and emphasize an attitude of the heart that submits to God. In the Mass, the Church requires the faithful to kneel during the consecration. However, in the United States this requirement is extended to include the entire Canon (a larger portion of the Mass surrounding the consecration).

Most churches in the United States and Canada have kneelers for the faithful. Some older churches in Europe lack kneelers, however, making standing the normal position during most liturgies.

Eucharistic Devotions

The Mass is the central prayer of the Church. The bread and wine offered at each Mass become the Body and Blood, Soul and Divinity of Jesus, the Second Person of the Holy Trinity. It is not surprising, then, that devotion should develop to worship God in the Blessed Sacrament outside of Mass. The Church is careful, however, to remind the faithful that any Eucharistic devotion should have its origin in the sacrifice of the Mass and should lead people back to the liturgy.

Four forms of Eucharistic devotion focus on the presence of Christ reserved in the Blessed Sacrament: *exposition, benediction, processions,* and *congresses.*

Exposition

Jesus in the Blessed Sacrament is reserved in tabernacles in churches around the world. Many Churches keep their doors open so that people can come to pray, not only in front of a statue or religious picture, but also in the presence of Jesus himself.

The Eucharist normally resides in the tabernacle, but to heighten awareness of the Blessed Sacrament, it can also be exposed to the view of the faithful during special times. A consecrated Host is placed in a *monstrance* so that it is visible to those who have come to pray. The monstrance is an ornate holder for the Blessed Sacrament used for exposition, benediction, and processions (see also below).

Exposition of the Blessed Sacrament may occur at specific times— for example, on the first Friday of each month, or daily from just after the completion of the morning Mass until sundown. Some churches and some religious congregations have *perpetual adoration* in front of the exposed Blessed Sacrament. In perpetual adoration, the Blessed Sacrament is only removed when Mass is being celebrated. Exposition allows private devotion before the actual presence of Jesus in the Host in the monstrance as a visual point of focus.

One traditional approach to Eucharistic exposition is the *Forty-Hour Devotion*. A parish chooses two days as a special time of exposition. The devotion begins and ends with a Mass. During the intervening time, the Eucharist is exposed around the clock.

The faithful make commitments to be present in consecutive periods of prayer so that our Lord is never alone, even through the night. When the apostles who accompanied Jesus to the Garden of Gethsemane fell asleep instead of praying with him, Jesus asked, "Could you not watch with me one hour?" (Mt 26:40). The Forty-Hour devotion gives us the opportunity to stay awake with Jesus and pray with him.

The closing Mass for the Forty-Hour Devotion is a solemn affair. Normally a procession winds through the church with the monstrance. It may even exit the church and continue through the neighborhood. Such a procession both honors Christ and proclaims the truth that he is truly present in the Host (see below).

Benediction

A benediction is a blessing, so *benediction* as a Eucharistic devotion is a blessing using the Blessed Sacrament. It occurs in the context of Eucharist exposition, usually at the end of a time of exposition.

Benediction begins with the priest placing the Blessed Sacrament on the altar for a time of devotion (if it is not already in place for adoration). A hymn of praise is sung, for example, the Latin Hymn "*O Salutaris Hostia*" ("O Saving Victim"). The priest incenses the Blessed Sacrament as the congregation prays quietly.

The time of adoration that follows may include communal hymns and prayers, as well as Scripture readings and a homily. After the period of prayer and adoration, the priest again incenses the Blessed Sacrament in the monstrance or ciborium. Again another Eucharist Hymn is sung, such as "*Tantum Ergo*" ("Sing, My Tongue, the Savior's Glory").

The priest then blesses the congregation with the Blessed Sacrament. While wearing the humeral veil, he holds the monstrance or ciborium aloft and makes the sign of the cross with it. The Divine Praises are often said while this blessing is given ("Blessed be God. Blessed be his holy name. Blessed be Jesus Christ, true God and true Man..."). After the blessing, the Eucharist is returned to the tabernacle to conclude the devotion.

Processions

In 1274 Pope Urban V established the feast of Corpus Christi ("the Body of Christ"). The Mass of this day, which celebrates Christ present in the Eucharist, gave impetus to many other devotions to the Blessed Sacrament. The Eucharistic *processions* that have traditionally occurred on the Feast of Corpus Christi, during Forty-Hour Devotion, and on other occasions became a source of devotional joy to many Catholics.

Ticker tape parades are one customary form of celebration when a dignitary comes to town or a victory has been won. The presence of

Jesus is far more worthy of a parade. A Eucharistic procession proclaims that Christ dwells with men through his unique presence in the Blessed Sacrament.

Typically, during a Eucharistic procession the Blessed Sacrament is placed in a monstrance so that the faithful can see the consecrated Host. The priest carries the monstrance using the humeral veil to demonstrate the sacredness of what he holds. Incense wafts heavenward, accompanied by the prayers of those in attendance. Eucharistic hymns are sung as the procession travels through the church or through the streets of the community. The devotion normally ends with benediction of the Blessed Sacrament.

Eucharistic Congresses

A *Eucharistic Congress* is part education, part devotion, and part proclamation. The First Eucharistic Congress was held in Lille, France, in 1873. The focus of a Eucharistic Congress is the celebration of the Mass by a large gathering of people. The gathering may be sponsored by a single diocese or by many dioceses on a national level or even internationally.

The congress includes teaching sessions on the nature of the Eucharist, as well as times for Confession, private prayer, and adoration before the Blessed Sacrament in exposition. The solemn liturgy for the Congress includes a procession.

Days That Make a Difference

The death and resurrection of Jesus are central tenets of the Catholic faith. From the beginning of the Church, Friday was honored as the day on which Christ died, while Sunday was honored as the day on which he rose. Before the yearly feasts of Good Friday and Easter Sunday were established, Christians celebrated every Friday and

Sunday as special days of prayer and remembrance. That tradition has continued down through the centuries.

Friday: Thankfulness and Repentance

Every Friday is to be a commemoration of the day that Jesus suffered and died. So Catholics are encouraged to make Friday a special day of prayer. It is appropriate to remember and give thanks for the salvation made available through the cross.

"God shows his love for us in that while we were yet sinners Christ died for us" (Rom 5:8). When contemplating both the great love of God and our own personal sin, the appropriate response is to repent of that sin, seek God's forgiveness, and ask his grace to live a more faithful and righteous life. Such repentance is not a once-in-a-lifetime event. Turning away from selfishness and sin, while turning to a merciful God, is the task of a lifetime. So Catholics are encouraged to focus on the continuing process of conversion especially on every Friday throughout the year.

In the past, the Church legislated specific rules for the observance of Friday. Prayer was encouraged and abstinence was required of all the faithful of appropriate age and health. (*Abstinence* normally means avoiding the consumption of meat.) This little sacrifice of abstaining from meat was an individual and corporate expression of the desire to put God first, a tangible expression of repentance and turning to God.

In 1966, however, the bishops of the United States relaxed the requirement of abstinence on Fridays. Since that time the practice has fallen into disuse among many Catholics. Nevertheless, the bishops reaffirmed the importance of keeping Friday as a day focused on repentance and conversion. They simply left the specific expression of penance to the discretion of the individual.

The bishops still encourage abstinence and fasting, while also encouraging good works such as visiting the sick, serving the needs of the elderly, and instructing the young—all as appropriate means of responding to God's call to conversion and heeding the gospel message. At present the Church in the United States requires abstinence only on the Fridays in Lent.

Sunday: A Day to Rise

For the Jews, the Sabbath—a weekly holy day of worship and rest—was celebrated on Saturday. The early Christians moved their weekly religious celebration from Saturday to Sunday because it was on that day that Jesus had risen from the dead. Thus on Sunday the Christians joined together for worship and the celebration of the Mass (see, for example, Acts 20:7).

The Ten Commandments had called for the Lord's Day (the Jewish Sabbath) to be kept holy (see Ex 20:8). Sunday became "the Lord's Day" for Christians (see Rv 1:10). Each Sunday is thus an opportunity to celebrate again the resurrection of Christ and to honor God. Each Sunday is a little celebration of Easter.

Christian Sunday worship has always included the celebration of the Eucharist. In fact, the Church obliges every Catholic to attend Mass on Sunday, if they are able to do so. This requirement is a reflection of the importance of worshiping God in a communal setting. It is part of the Catholic way to keep the Sabbath holy.

The Church also encourages Catholics to observe Sunday as a day of rest, prayer, and a time for spiritual growth and study. Pope John Paul II, in the apostolic letter "On Keeping the Lord's Day Holy," identifies Sunday as a "family" day. First, he notes, the local Catholic community gathers as family to share the Eucharist. In addition, individual families should "share a few formative and reflective moments." Catholics are to spend Sunday "in such a way that the peace and joy of the Risen Lord will emerge in the ordinary events of life ... family life, social relationships, moments of relaxation."[2]

Music: Praying Twice

St. Augustine said that "to sing is to pray twice." The words of a song may be a vocal prayer, while the music, in its best form, raises the mind and heart in joy to contemplate the highest ideals.

Music has been an important part of worship in our religious tradition since the time of the Old Testament. The Jews sang the psalms. So we know that Jesus used music in prayer, as he would have prayed the psalms according to Jewish custom. In addition, we have references in the New Testament to Jesus and the apostles praying and singing a hymn (see Mt 26:30); St. Paul and St. Silas praying and singing a hymn (see Acts 16:25); and the early Christians singing when they gathered to pray, worship, and celebrate the Eucharist (see 1 Cor 14:26; Eph 5:19; Col 3:16).

When the Catholic bishops of the United States set the current guidelines for liturgical music in 1972, they used the theme of love to characterize the value of music in worship: "People in love make signs of love, not only to express their love but also to deepen it."[3] Music in worship, whether instrumental or sung, is an expression and deepening of love for God.

Not all music is suitable for liturgy in the Church. Music must be faith-based. In a liturgical context, it must not be a performance; rather, it should assist and encourage the congregation in worship and growth in faith.

To ensure the appropriateness of music within a liturgical setting the bishops of the United States have established a threefold test to judge whether particular music is to be considered for liturgical use: the *musical* judgment, the *liturgical* judgment, and the *pastoral* judgment. Other bishops' conferences around the world have established similar directives for use in their particular jurisdictions.

The Musical Judgment

Music in the liturgy should be of high quality, meaning that the technical, expressive, and aesthetic aspects of the music should be very good. Liturgical music is prayer and thus an offering to God. The Scripture of the Old Covenant is specific that what is offered to God should be pure and without defect (see Ex 39).

The Liturgical Judgment

Music is to enhance the liturgy and not detract from it. A song that is appropriate for the processional may not be right for the offertory. An Advent song probably would be out of place at Easter. In addition, the type and style of music should correspond to the relative importance of various parts of the liturgy.

The words of a song are also important. They, too, should correspond to the liturgical setting, and they should conform to sound Christian doctrine. In this regard, texts drawn from Scripture are encouraged.

The Pastoral Judgment

Any element in the liturgy must work for the spiritual well-being of the congregation. The goal is to help people focus on God, draw near to him, and be open to his grace. Any decisions about music in the liturgy must answer in the affirmative this question: "Does [the] music in the celebration enable these people to express their faith, in this place, in this age, in this culture?"[4]

Music at Mass

Music is encouraged in certain parts of the Mass. In other parts of the Mass, while not encouraged, it is permitted. In all cases the music must meet the musical, liturgical, and pastoral tests before use is permitted.

Five acclamations "ought to be sung"[5]:

The *Alleluia* (Gospel acclamation)

The *Sanctus* ("Holy, Holy, Holy Lord ...")

The *Memorial Acclamation* after the Consecration (for example, "Christ has died, Christ is risen, Christ will come again")

The *Great Amen* at the end of the Canon

The *Doxology of the Lord's Prayer* ("for the kingdom, the power, and the glory are yours, now and forever")

These acclamations are shouts of joy in response to key aspects of the liturgy. Therefore, it is proper to sing them. In fact, the Alleluia before the reading of the gospel is to be omitted if it is not sung.

Processional songs are used as an entrance song and for Communion. This type of song mirrors the "Songs of Ascent" found in the Old Testament Psalms, which focused on the trip to the temple in Jerusalem and into God's presence. The processional songs at Mass proclaim that the congregation is coming into God's presence.

After the first reading comes a *responsorial psalm* taken from the Psalms. The singing of the responsorial psalm continues the Jewish tradition of chanting these scriptural texts.

The parts of the Mass that may be sung include these:

The *Kyrie* ("Lord, Have Mercy")

The *Gloria* ("Glory to God in the highest ...")

The Creed ("I believe in God ...")

The Our Father

The *Agnus Dei* ("O Lamb of God ...")

Hymns may also be used during the preparation of the gifts at the Offertory, after Communion as a focus for reflection, and as the recessional at the end of Mass.

Gregorian Chant

Certain music and musical settings are part of the treasury of Catholic worship. For example, although various instruments may be used in a liturgical setting, the organ has come to assume a preeminent place.

In addition, although many musical styles are acceptable, Gregorian chant maintains a special place in liturgical music. The word *chant* comes from a Latin word meaning "to sing." In the early Middle Ages several types of chants were used: Ambrosian, Galliean, Mozarabic, and others. The Roman form of chant, however, came to dominate. Pope Gregory I (560–604) is credited with promoting the use of chant in the liturgy, and today it bears his name: *Gregorian* chant.

Marian Devotion

Mary, the mother of Jesus, has been held in honor among Christians since the early centuries. She was a witness to the life, death, and resurrection of Christ. She was there when the Holy Spirit descended on the apostles at Pentecost and the Church began to grow in power.

Jesus' mother has occupied a place of honor in the Church from the very beginning. There are depictions of her in the catacombs, the burial place of early Christians in Rome. St. Ignatius, who died between the years 98 and 117, wrote about the perpetual virginity of the Blessed Mother.

St. Irenaeus, who lived in the second century and has been called the first Marian theologian, described Mary as the New Eve. Both Mary and Eve, he insisted, were virgins who gave life to a new order: "As mankind was bound to death through a virgin [Eve], it is saved through a virgin [Mary]; by the obedience of a virgin the disobedience of a virgin is compensated."[6]

By the fifth century there were three feasts in the Church's liturgical calendar to celebrate Mary. Thus from the earliest days of the Church, she was honored and her intercession was sought.

The fact that Mary was a virgin when she gave birth to Jesus is recognized in the Apostles' Creed with the clause "born of the virgin Mary." Other Marian teachings, such as the Assumption or the Immaculate Conception, can be found in "seed" form in the early Church.

This is not to say that the Church developed a full Marian theology in its early history. The Church grew in the understanding of these truths only over time. But it was not a matter of novel doctrines being added, as some would insist. Rather, the Church, in reflection over centuries, eventually gave definition to truths that were in some form acknowledged from the beginning.

Devotion to Mary consists of three elements. First, there is the acknowledgement of who Mary is in the plan of salvation.

She was conceived without the stain of sin as a worthy vessel to bear the Son of God. As a young woman she freely gave her assent to become the Mother of God, Jesus. She lived a holy and obedient life as a witness to the life, death, and resurrection of Christ, and she was assumed into heaven as a witness to the bodily resurrection that is promised to all in the redemption won by Christ. Preeminent among the saints, Mary intercedes for those who are children of the Father and brothers and sisters of Jesus—and thus her children as well.

From this understanding of Mary's nature and role, the Church has always encouraged the faithful to honor her. Honor is due to all the saints who have been faithful in following Christ. The Greek term *dulia* refers to this honor.

As the first among saints, Mary is to be honored above all the others. So the honor given her is called *hyperdulia*—that is, primary or highest honor. But Church theologians such as St. Augustine and St. Thomas Aquinas have been careful to distinguish the honor due to the saints and to Mary, in particular, from the worship that is due to God alone. This worship of God is called in the Greek *latria,* and only God is worthy of it.

Catholics honor Mary by signs of devotion and prayer. May crowning, Marian shrines, and various Marian prayers such as the Litany of Loretto and the Angelus are all means of showing honor to Mary. In showing honor to Mary, Catholics not only acknowledge her special place in salvation history; they also imitate Jesus, who honored and obeyed his mother.

We identify a second key element in Marian devotion when we acknowledge her as a means of drawing closer to Christ. She always pointed to her Son, and she calls us to that same focus. As the Mother of God, Mary presented Jesus to the world at birth. She took part in the very beginning of Jesus' public ministry as she encouraged his first miracle at the wedding feast in Cana (see Jn 2:1-11). At his death she stood at the foot of the cross and directed her gaze to her Son, the Savior.

Leading men and women to Christ is a mission that Mary still fulfills today. To go to Mary and meditate on her life is to be led to her Son, Jesus. To look to Jesus through the eyes and heart of Mary is to come to an appreciation of both the divine and the human natures of Christ. Mary is not the end or goal of devotion. She is a pure channel to God.

The third element of devotion to Mary is asking for her intercession. Since she belongs to the communion of saints, Mary can pray for us. So Catholics often have recourse to her as a partner in prayer.

Mary not only is the greatest of saints; she also has the heart of a mother for us, her children. From the cross, Jesus entrusted Mary to the beloved disciple, John, as mother (see Jn 19:26-27). In this action Catholics see Mary given to all disciples as mother. When prayer requests are entrusted to Mary, they are entrusted to the heart of a mother who cherishes and desires the best for her children.

Apparitions

Appearances of Mary have been reported throughout the history of the Church. Belief in these apparitions—even those the Church has approved as worthy of belief—is not required of Catholics. However, the Church does provide guidance concerning the messages of such apparitions.

The messages Mary is reported to have given in approved apparitions all have the same basic theme. They call for conversion and greater love of her Son, the Son of God, Jesus. Many Marian devotions have arisen from these apparitions in such places as Tepayac, Mexico (Our Lady of Guadalupe); Lourdes, France; and Fatima, Portugal, to name only a few.

Mary was the one who brought Jesus into the world two thousand years ago. In her many apparitions, she continues to bring Jesus and his message to the world.

Heavenly Prayer Partners: the Saints

Saints—those who have preceded us to heaven and now dwell with God, where they contemplate and praise him—still have work to do. The Church teaches that the intercessory prayers of the saints are "their most exalted service in God's plan."[7] All Catholics are therefore encouraged to keep the saints on the job by asking them to "intercede for us and for the whole world."[8]

Canonization

In particular, intercession is sought from *canonized* saints. A canonized saint is someone recognized by the Church as having attained heaven, who now dwells with God. Saints were recognized in this way from the very beginning of the Church. Early martyrs, who had shed their blood as a witness to Christ, were honored, and their intercession was sought. Up until about the tenth century, saints were recognized by popular acclamation. Eventually, the Church established a process to verify the sanctity of the individual before formally recognizing the person as a saint.

The current procedure for recognizing a saint was established by Pope John Paul II in 1983 and was a modification of the procedure in effect prior to that date. According to the present guidelines, five years must have passed since the date of death of the candidate before the process leading to canonization can begin. The bishop of the diocese where the person died is responsible for beginning the investigation of the individual.

Local authorities in the diocese collect information about the candidate, and they examine the person's life to see whether the individual exercised heroic virtue. All writings by and about the candidate are collected and examined. This information is then submitted to an agency of the Vatican, the *Congregation for the Causes of Saints.* If there is a positive response to the initial investigation, the individual is declared to be a "Servant of God."

The Vatican congregation continues to examine the life of the individual and calls witnesses to testify about the person. Before the candidate can move to the next step in the process, a miracle must be attributed to his or her intercession. The miracle must have occurred after the death of the individual and must be rigorously investigated and verified. When these criteria are met, the cause is submitted to the pope, who can then declare the person as "Blessed."

Many of those investigated for sainthood may not progress beyond the first two stages. For them to complete the canonization process, one more miracle must be attributed to the candidate, and this miracle must occur after the individual has been declared "Blessed." Again, the purported miracle is closely examined. There can be no natural explanation for the miracle, and it must be shown that it is directly linked to the intercession of the particular candidate in question.

If a miracle is verified, the cause again is submitted to the pope, who makes the final decision. Only after that process and final approval is the person declared a "saint." Once that happens, the day assigned to celebrate the feast of the saint is usually the date of the anniversary of the person's death—the date the person was born to eternal life in heaven.

Intercession

One key to the canonization process is the verification of a miracle that occurred through the intercession of the candidate for sainthood. As we have already noted, saints offer effective prayers for us before the throne of God, and verification of that reality in the case of a particular departed Christian is essential to his or her canonization.

To intercede is to go between two parties and plead on behalf of one party before the other party. The Council of Trent taught that saints offer prayers to God on behalf of men and women. The council also declared that it was of value to ask for the prayer and aid of the saints to obtain benefits from God through Jesus Christ. The benefit comes from Christ who alone is Redeemer, Savior, and Lord. Nevertheless, the saint is the party in the middle who speaks on our behalf.

Isn't it easier merely to pray directly to God and skip the intermediary? Certainly we can and should pray directly to God. However, Christianity is more than merely a "me and God" affair.

Scripture regularly refers to the communal nature of faith. Christ established a Church, a body of believers. When one member of that body suffers, the effects are felt by all. When one member rejoices, all rejoice. The sins of one weaken the body, while the heroic virtue of others (such as the canonized saints) positively impacts the life and effectiveness of all believers.

Prayers of intercession to the saints reflect this reality, the *communion of saints*. We are all linked together under Christ as our Head.

Praying for one another is encouraged in Scripture. For example, St. Paul asked for prayers from the Church: "Strive together with me in your prayers to God on my behalf" (Rom 15:30). The prayers of the saints in heaven are particularly effective because saints are close to God. As St. Jerome observed: "If the apostles and martyrs, while still in the body, can pray for others, at a time when they must be anxious for themselves, how much more after their crowns, victories, and triumphs are won!"[9]

Guardian Angels

Angels are spiritual beings existing along the continuum between God and man. They are created beings, like humans, but they have no physical bodies. The English word *angel* comes from the Latin word for "messenger," which is one of their roles.

Scripture provides various examples of angels sent to give divine messages to men and women on earth. For example, the angel Gabriel came to Mary to announce to her that she would be the mother of the promised Savior (see Lk 1:26-38).

However, the primary duty of angels is to attend God and worship him. Biblical texts refer to angels as standing before God's throne (see Rv 8:2-5). They worship God and are ever ready to do his divine bidding.

The Church teaches that God has directed angels to help and protect humans. They certainly can intercede for us, just as do the saints. Yet their ministry to us goes deeper and perhaps is more personal.

Angels have a certain guardianship over us. In the Gospel of Matthew, Jesus speaks about those who would lead others into sin. In this context, he says: "See that you do not despise one of these little ones; for I tell you that in heaven their angels always behold the face of my Father who is in heaven" (Mt 18:10).

From this scriptural text and from a long tradition, the concept of *guardian angels* has developed. This teaching is not a defined article of faith for the Catholic. But it is a treasured tradition that God has assigned an angel to watch over every man and woman as a help in this earthly journey, with all its struggles and difficulties.

It is a pious practice to acknowledge regularly the presence of our guardian angel and to ask specifically for the angel's help and protection. In particular, Catholics ask their guardian angels to enlighten and guide them and to help them resist temptation and evil. The feast of the Guardian Angels is celebrated every year on October 2.

Praying for the Dead

St. Paul tells us that love endures because it is eternal (see 1 Cor 13:8-13). Love is neither ended nor even hindered by death, so it effectively reaches beyond the grave. It is a comfort to Catholics to know that their ties of love to those who have died are maintained. The saints in heaven can pray for those still living on earth, and we on earth can pray for those who are in purgatory.

God's grace is available in superabundance for all men and women. However, the door to that grace can be opened wider by the prayers and good works of believers. The faithful are all connected in the communion of saints. We have the same Father in heaven and the same elder brother in Jesus.

Think of an electric grid. If you put the right type of wire in place on one part of the grid, the electricity will flow more freely to the other parts of the grid. The wire doesn't create the energy; it merely is a conduit.

In a similar way, individuals in the body of Christ don't create grace, but by prayer and good works they can be a conduit of grace. Prayers can be offered to help those in purgatory during their time of purification.

It is worth noting that only those in the process of purification can benefit from this prayer. Those in heaven do not need prayer because they enjoy fullness of life in God's presence. Nothing could be added to their happiness and well-being.

At the same time, it would be useless to pray for the damned. They have chosen to reject God and thus have removed themselves from the communion of saints and from the life-giving grace that flows through the body of Christ.

The practice of praying for the deceased has a long tradition in the Church and in the Jewish community in which the Church was born. Scripture tells us that the ancient Jews prayed for their comrades slain in battle (see 2 Mac 12:39-45). Prayers for departed Christians can be found in early inscriptions in the catacombs.

Evidence that the faithful departed were remembered in the prayers of the Mass is found in early liturgical texts as well. Christian writers, at least from the time of the second century, give witness to the practice of praying for the deceased on the anniversary of their death.

Prayers can be prayed for the faithful departed at any time. The prayer can focus either on specific individuals or on the departed in general.

Indulgences

Some Catholic traditions are widely understood and appreciated by Catholics and non-Catholics alike. However, other traditions are often misunderstood. Indulgences certainly fall into the latter category. So it may be helpful to start this discussion with an official definition.

Pope Paul VI wrote:

An indulgence is a remission before God of the temporal punishment due to sins whose guilt has already been forgiven, which the faithful Christian who is duly disposed gains under certain prescribed conditions through the action of the Church which, as the minister of redemption, dispenses and applies with authority the treasury of the satisfactions of Christ and the saints.[10]

Let's look at several key elements in this definition.

Temporal Punishment

An indulgence does not grant forgiveness of sin. Normally, serious sin is forgiven through the sacrament of Reconciliation. However, as we noted earlier, sin has consequences, even sin that has been forgiven.

Temporal punishment refers to these consequences of sin. Sin wounds a person. Mortal sin seriously injures a person. The grace of Confession forgives the sin and saves the life of the person, but a wound remains that needs to be healed.

The healing from temporal punishment can occur in this life through ongoing conversion, prayer, and the good works of the person whose sins have been forgiven. It can take place through the purification after death in purgatory. It can also be aided through indulgences as dispensed from the treasury of the Church.

A Wealth of Grace

Christ gave authority to his disciples and to all their followers when he established the Church to carry on his work on earth. In particular, he gave his disciples the power of the "keys" when he told them: "I will give you the keys of the kingdom of heaven, and whatever you bind on earth shall be bound in heaven, and whatever you loose on earth shall be loosed in heaven" (Mt 16:19). In this way Jesus established the sacrament of Reconciliation and, by extension, the authority to dispense indulgences to deal with the temporal punishment of sins.

The financial concept of trust funds provides a helpful analogy. A wealthy entrepreneur can establish a trust fund for the care of his child. He can then appoint an administrator to oversee the distribution of the fund.

In a similar way, God has established a great treasury of grace and appointed the Church, in the person of the pope, to distribute its wealth. The pope is the earthly administrator with the authority to distribute those treasures for the care and blessing of God's children.

That treasury of grace consists primarily of the merits of the death and resurrection of Christ. Added to these are the prayers and good works of the saints, especially those of the greatest of saints, Mary, the Mother of God.

Indulgences release the individual from temporal punishment—from captivity to the consequences of sin. As Pope John Paul II has emphasized, Jesus is the ultimate source of this grace: "The starting point for understanding indulgences is the abundance of God's mercy revealed in the Cross of Christ. The crucified Jesus is the great 'indulgence' that the Father has offered humanity through the forgiveness of sins and the possibility of living as children in the Holy Spirit."[11]

Jesus sets people free. The Church he founded continues that practice and uses indulgences as one of its tools to heal and liberate them.

How to Get an Indulgence

Only the pope can determine indulgences with universal application. Bishops have certain authority within their jurisdictions to set guidelines for local indulgenced acts or prayers. Details are provided in a manual, the *Enchiridion Indulgentiarum*, which lists those acts and prayers that can carry indulgences. The most recent version of this manual was published in 1968; an addendum was added in 1999, with specific indulgences made available for the Jubilee year of 2000.

An example of an action that could qualify for obtaining an indulgence is "a visit to a Church or altar on the day of its consecration" or a "visit to a cemetery." Prayers that may have an indulgence attached include various litanies, some novenas, and specific prayers such as the Magnificat.[12]

Indulgences are not magic, so they are not automatically conferred upon an individual upon performance of the associated action. In general, there are five key requirements for receiving an indulgence:

1. Reception of sacramental Confession (sin needs to be forgiven before the temporal punishment can be addressed).
2. Reception of the Eucharist.
3. Prayer for the intentions of the Holy Father (the pope).
4. At least a general intention to obtain the indulgence.
5. Absence of attachment to sin.

Indulgences come in two types: *partial* or *plenary*. A plenary indulgence gives remission of all temporal punishment, while a partial indulgence removes only a portion.

Sometimes a partial indulgence will state a number of days as the period of remission (such as "sixty days" or "ninety days"). This does not refer to some period of time in purgatory from which the recipient of the indulgence has been exempt. Rather, it refers to the number of days of penance in this life for which the indulgence has an equivalent value. Primarily, the term "days" serves to show the relative value of various activities and prayers.

The disposition of the individual also affects the reception of the indulgence. If we are truly detached from sin, then the remission of the temporal punishment can be greater than for someone who is less disposed to receive the grace.

We can obtain indulgences either for ourselves or for the faithful departed.

Abuse

The Church is careful to teach that indulgences are not magic and that they are not a license to live a sinful life. Pope John Paul II stated that indulgences are not a "discount" on the duty of conversion and living a Christian life. They must be more than the mere performance of outward acts. Instead, he observes, the outward acts required for an indulgence "are required as the expression of ... conversion. They particularly show our faith in God's mercy."[13]

Misuse of indulgences helped to provoke the Protestant Reformation. In some instances indulgences were "sold," or at least appeared to be sold, as a means to raise funds for building churches and other activities. This was an obvious abuse of the doctrine and was corrected at the Council of Trent.

The teaching about indulgences, however, was the same before and after the Council of Trent. In fact, even though some who represented the Church at the time presented indulgences in an inappropriate manner, those who fulfilled the normal requirements still received the indulgences validly.

Recent popes have reaffirmed the use of indulgences. In 1967 Pope Paul VI wrote an apostolic constitution on indulgences that serves as the modern reference for understanding the practice and the theology behind it. Pope John Paul II as well has written on several occasions concerning the use and value of indulgences.

Blessings

The dictionary gives three definitions for the verb "to bless." The first meaning is "to consecrate," that is, to set something aside for a special, holy use. "To invoke divine care" is the second definition. "The conferring of happiness or prosperity" is the third definition.

Who has the power and authority to consecrate, to provide care, to bring prosperity—to bless? Only God has that power, and the Scriptures contain many examples of his blessing being imparted. In fact, to bless seems to be a primary function of God's love. For example, after God created in the beginning, he blessed his creation (see Gn 1–2).

All blessings come from God. However, not every blessing comes *directly* from God. Christ established a Church to carry on his ministry on earth. He gave authority to his disciples to work in his name, power, and authority. The Church and her ministers use this authority to administer blessings.

As we have noted, objects officially blessed by the Church become sacramentals. Blessings can also be bestowed upon people. There is a blessing for pilgrims, a blessing for engaged couples, a blessing for expectant mothers, and many more.

An agent of the Church administers the blessing. The minister may be a priest or deacon. The minister can even be a layperson who acts in the authority of the Church in a particular situation. God's grace and the prayers of the entire Church underlie the blessing. The effectiveness of a blessing, however, is dependent upon the openness of the recipient of the blessing.

Blessings of an unofficial nature can also be given by someone in a position of God-given authority. For example, parents are placed in authority over their children, and part of the grace of the sacrament of marriage is the grace to be an effective spouse and parent. So parents can bless their children—a prayer that is heard and honored by God.

Offer It Up

Self-denial and sacrifice can be a part of prayer. For example, fasting and abstinence—two kinds of personal sacrifice we have already discussed—are a source of grace when combined with right intention and prayer.

Many other acts of self-denial can assist a person in prayer. Rising from bed on time, refraining from speaking an angry word, and doing some act of kindness to help someone else are all examples of small sacrifices that can aid in prayer. Though these actions may sometimes be meaningless in themselves, with the right intention they can be powerful aids in drawing closer to God.

A young man may tell a young woman that he loves her, but when he also buys her a small gift, it adds something to the expression of love. The extra effort involved in buying that gift can also deepen the intensity of love within the young man.

Sacrifice adds the same dimensions to prayer. It says to God: "I am serious about loving you and obeying you. I am so serious that I am willing to sacrifice my own convenience for you." Acts of self-denial also have an effect on the person who performs them since they cement the commitment to God with action.

These acts of sacrifice can be performed for specific intentions. For example: "Lord, I am getting up early this morning to pray, and I specifically ask that by your grace I will grow in the virtue of patience." Or the sacrifice can be offered for someone else: "Lord, I am willing to endure this inconvenience of waiting in line, and I offer it for the intention of my sister who is in the hospital."

From this practice comes an exhortation familiar to most Catholics: "Offer it up!" It seems to be an appropriate expression for offering a sacrifice up to God as prayer.

In Perspective

Self-denial and sacrifice can be helps in prayer, but they can also be abused. God does not will for us to suffer needlessly. He does desire that we grow closer to him and seek what is most important in life: a relationship with him.

Self-sacrifices should be vehicles for prayer and growth. While encouraging fasting and other forms of mortification, the Church has always cautioned against overzealous practices.

As we have seen, the Catholic faith has a rich tradition of prayer—the turning of the mind and heart to God, not just through thoughts and words but also through attitudes and habits, postures and actions, music and art. Whether we pray alone, with the saints and angels, or with the Church in the liturgy, we draw close to our Creator—and advance farther along the way that leads us home to be with him forever.

FIVE

Trends and Developments

The Catholic Church provides an interesting study in contrasts. On the one hand, she appears never to change. In fact, the core of the faith has remained intact for two thousand years. The Church maintains that the revealed truths of the faith cannot be changed. These truths are protected and passed on from one generation to the next. Though our understanding of the truths may develop over time, and their application to particular situations may show some variation, the essentials remain constant.

Nevertheless, the Catholic Church also shows a significant amount of variation in practice and custom. The Church is worldwide and has shown the ability to embrace many cultures. Ethnic practices of Catholics in Albania can be very different from those of Catholics in Mexico. Yet the Church can handle the differences.

This book has focused primarily on the Western or Latin Church. Catholics of the Eastern rites, such as the Byzantine or Maronite, have liturgies that, while the same as the Latin in essentials, use different expressions and emphasis in practice.

Additionally, some changes in custom and tradition occur over time. Certainly many traditions have a long history. However, others have come and gone.

Liturgical Changes

Prior to Vatican II the Mass in the Western Church was basically the same whether it was said in the Philippines or in Ireland. The Mass was everywhere said in Latin, and there was very little variation in the way it was said.

With Vatican II came adjustments. While retaining the option for the Mass in Latin, the opportunity for saying the Mass in the language of the country or region became possible. Some flexibility was added in the prayers that could be chosen. Local conferences of bishop were given some latitude to decide on how the liturgy could incorporate local customs.

Today, on a given Sunday, a single parish church in the United States may have one Mass in English, another in Spanish, and a third in Korean. There are Masses in which the music is Gregorian chant, and Masses with guitars and modern folk music to lead people in worship. The traditional Tridentine liturgy in use before Vatican II could be used in a church for a morning Mass, while later in the day a particular liturgy might include the exuberant praise that characterizes the charismatic renewal.

Despite all these variations acceptable today, however, the essence of the Mass remains the same as it was when the first Mass was celebrated on the night Jesus was betrayed. Bread and wine are changed into the Body and Blood, the Soul and Divinity of Christ. The sacrifice of Calvary is again made manifest on the altar, and Jesus gives himself as spiritual food to the congregation.

Many changes have been made in the liturgy of the Catholic Church over the past forty years in particular. There have even been changes made in some of the changes! However, when the Second Vatican Council was opening the doors to change, the council fathers were careful to implement guidelines for how that change would occur. The *Constitution on the Sacred Liturgy* was published in 1963 and provides the framework for developments in the liturgy.

According to the council's instructions, two key criteria guide all liturgical changes. First, change should not be undertaken purely for the sake of change: "There must be no innovations unless the good of the Church genuinely and certainly requires them."[1]

Second, changes should not be radical. Rather, they should develop from a growth in the understanding of the historic liturgy within the culture or society. The council fathers wrote: "Care must be taken that any new forms adopted should in some way grow organically from forms already existing."[2]

The Laity

One notable change in recent years has been a greater involvement of the laity in the Mass and in other liturgies. Laymen and women can now serve as lectors, readers, and extraordinary ministers of the Eucharist. The congregation also has greater active participation in the liturgy through responses and music.

Even so, the laity is not to replace the ordained clergy. The ordained clergy—bishops, priests, and deacons—continue to have the primary liturgical and preaching roles in the Church. Recent popes have cautioned against a "clericalization" of the laity. Though the laity can be more involved in the liturgies of the Church, the primary role of laymen and women is not liturgical. Rather, the laity is to take the good news out into the world and serve as Christian "leaven" in that world.

Pope John Paul II has often emphasized this aspect of the role of the laity: "The premier place of the exercise of the lay vocation is in the world of economic, social, political, and cultural realities. It is in this world that lay people are called to live their baptismal vocation."[3]

New Liturgical Customs

Many new liturgical customs have developed over the past forty years. The sacrament of Reconciliation can now be received face to face. The funeral liturgy focuses more on the aspects of resurrection and hope; the normal color of the vestments is now white instead of black.

The communal aspects of the Mass have also received greater emphasis. Responses are corporate as well as individual. The Mass is not only where the individual encounters Christ; it is also where God ministers to his people, his family.

This sense of community has always been a part of the Church's understanding. However, it has been more fully developed in recent times. This development has given rise to new expressions within the Mass. The *sign of peace,* for example, has been added officially to the liturgy. Other expressions that have become common in some places—such as holding hands during the praying of the Our Father—are not officially a part of the liturgy.

New Customs in Other Sacraments

New customs have developed in the celebration of some of the other sacraments as well. For example, the exchange of rings has been a common feature in marriages for decades. However, the practice of the unity candle is a new development that has spread significantly in popular usage.

In this practice, two candles are lit prior to the wedding. These candles represent the individual lives of the bride and groom. After the marriage ceremony, the bride and groom take the individual candles and light one new candle as a symbol of their new life together. Then they extinguish the first two candles.

This custom is a wonderful symbol of the unity of marriage. But even though it has become popular, it is not a part of the official wedding liturgy. It is merely a new and popular custom.

New Devotions

New devotions arise in various ways in the Church. New movements, religious orders, and institutions bring fresh expressions to Catholic spirituality. The charismatic renewal in the Catholic Church, for example, has a particular type of spirituality emphasizing openness to the gifts of the Holy Spirit. Predominantly lay movements such as Focolare, Communion and Liberation, Opus Dei, and the Legionaries of Christ have drawn many to their particular forms of prayer and devotion. Some of these newer movements are gaining adherents, while older religious orders such as the Jesuits, Benedictines, Dominicans, and Franciscans have declined in numbers.

Numerous new saints, such as Edith Stein and Padre Pio, have been canonized during the pontificate of Pope John Paul II. These recently canonized saints bring new intercessors and examples of holiness into the life of the Church. Devotion to them has generated new prayer movements and study groups. For example, Padre Pio prayer groups now exist in many parts of the world.

Divine Mercy

In 2000 Pope John Paul II canonized a Polish nun by the name of Sr. Faustina, who had died in 1938. In this act, the Church gave official blessing to a new devotion and established a new feast, Divine Mercy Sunday. An examination of the events that preceded the canonization provides insight into one way in which new devotions enter into the life of the Church.

Sr. Faustina was a young Polish nun who claimed to be receiving private revelations from Jesus. She kept a journal of the messages she received. According to the journal, on fourteen occasions Jesus appeared to this sister.

As a bit of background, we should note that the public revelations that are part of the faith deposit of the Church ended with the apostles. However, the Church recognizes that individuals may still receive private revelations. Even so, the Church must always approach private revelations, such as those of Sr. Faustina, with caution. In determining the authenticity of such revelations, the character of the recipient and the orthodoxy of the messages must first be closely examined by the local church officials.

Belief in any private revelation is not demanded by the Church. But once the Church has examined a private revelation, it is often able to give a determination as to its worthiness or value. For example, a Catholic is free to believe or disbelieve in the apparitions at Lourdes and at Fatima. Nevertheless, the Church has pronounced that the messages of these two apparitions are consistent with Catholic teaching and recommends their acceptance by the faithful.

Since the messages received by Sr. Faustina were private revelations, they had to undergo the scrutiny of the Church. These messages focused on the mercy of God that is available especially through the sacraments of the Eucharist and Reconciliation. Faustina said that God wanted an annual Feast of Mercy to be established and that, on this feast, his mercy would be available in a special way to those who humbly and faithfully received the sacraments of the Eucharist and Reconciliation.

Sr. Faustina also said Jesus requested that a painting be created to depict his mercy. She gave specific details for how it should be composed. The journal of this nun included as well specific prayers that focused on the Divine Mercy.

The first of the messages to Sr. Faustina occurred in 1931. The Divine Mercy image was painted in 1934. In October of 1938 Sr. Faustina died and was buried in Krakow, Poland.

Among a relatively small group of Catholics in Poland, devotion to

Christ in his Divine Mercy began to grow. The image was venerated and a new chaplet and novena prayers were used. The devotion spread from Poland to other parts of the world, often through Polish immigrants. At the same time, the life and message of Sr. Faustina came under examination.

The Divine Mercy message was finally give approbation by the Church as not contrary to Church teaching, and the merits of the life of Sr. Faustina were noted. In 1993 she was beatified (declared "Blessed"). This act gave a greater impetus to the Divine Mercy devotion as more people became aware of the messages.

In 1997, Pope John Paul II visited the burial site of Sr. Faustina and announced his personal devotion to Jesus in his Divine Mercy. Finally, on April 30, 2000, Sr. Faustina was canonized. At the same time the Holy Father declared that the Sunday after Easter would be celebrated as Divine Mercy Sunday.

Thus in a period of seventy years a devotion that had been prompted by a private revelation became a feast in the universal liturgical year. We should note, of course, that the Divine Mercy message teaches nothing new. It is consistent with the Catholic understanding of Christ, his mission, and the sacraments. However, through this devotion the reality of God's mercy has received a new emphasis and focus.

Christ, the Goal

As we look back over the rich variety of Catholic customs, one challenge we face in the twenty-first century is to continue to find significance in expressions that may be centuries old. What do the customs and traditions of the Church mean to us personally? Can they still have relevance in the twenty-first century?

The purpose of this book has been to cultivate a deeper understanding of Catholic spiritual traditions. Such understanding can help us in several ways. In some cases, we are able to discover anew the meaning of a particular custom so we can use it in a fresh way to express or experience the love between God and his people. In other cases, understanding traditions creates an appreciation of the lives and loves of those who have preceded us in history even while helping us develop new, meaningful customs to express spiritual reality in the context of contemporary culture.

As we seek this richer understanding, we should always keep in mind that all the customs and traditions discussed in this book have one goal: to deepen our relationship with God. Some are essential in that task, such as Baptism. Others, such as scapulars, can be helpful, but they are not essential. Some traditions can be traced back to Christ, while others are of recent vintage. Yet whatever their origin and relative importance, the Catholic Church provides a vital role in preserving what is of value in them, cautioning when abuse is possible, and teaching that eternal life in Christ is always their goal.

Notes

One
Living a Spiritual Life

1. *Code of Canon Law*, 891.
2. "Decree on Age of Confirmation from USCCB," August 21, 2001.
3. *Catechism of the Catholic Church* (hereafter cited as "CCC") 1285.
4. CCC 1300.
5. *Lumen Gentium*, 11; see Nicholas Halligan, O.P., *The Sacraments and their Celebration* (New York: Alba, 1986), 53.
6. "Celebration" is a correct term. Some find confession of sins difficult. However, it is a great joy to be forgiven!
7. There is no formula mandated for the universal Church. However, various dioceses or regional areas may have mandated a formula for their jurisdiction.
8. CCC 1628.
9. Pius XII, encyclical *Mediator Dei*, 39.
10. See the entry for "Celibacy" in Peter M.J. Stravinskas, ed., *Our Sunday Visitor's Catholic Dictionary* (Huntington, Ind.: Our Sunday Visitor, 1993), 122.
11. A permanent deacon is differentiated from a transitional deacon. A transitional deacon is in a process that will lead to ordination as a priest.
12. See the entry "Extreme Unction" in the 1917 edition of *The Catholic Encyclopedia*, available online at www.newadvent.org/cathen.
13. CCC 1511.
14. Paul VI, apostolic constitution *Sacram Unctionem Informorum*, 1972.
15. At death the soul of the faithful departed is united with God. At the end of time the soul and the glorified body will be reunited to

live with God and all the saints in a "new heaven and a new earth" (see Rv 21:1).

Two
Times and Seasons

1. Dionysius of Alexander (c. A.D. 260) writes about the six days of fasting that preceded the celebration of Easter.
2. See the discussion of holy water in chapter three, "Sacramentals and Signs."
3. From the Preface of the Holy Eucharist.
4. In fact, body and soul will be reunited in the resurrection of the body at the end of time.
5. From the Easter Proclamation *(Exsultet)* of the Easter Vigil.
6. CCC 638.
7. From the Preface for Easter.
8. From the Sequence for Easter Mass during the day.
9. See the entry on "Pentecost (Jewish Feast)" in the 1914 edition of *The Catholic Encyclopedia,* online at www.newadvent.org/cathen.
10. Alternate opening prayer for Trinity Sunday.
11. This is the technical term for the transformation that occurs at each Mass in which the substances of bread and wine are changed into the Body and Blood of Christ while retaining the appearances of bread and wine.
12. Stanzas 5 and 6 from the sequence for the Feast of Corpus Christi.
13. A *monstrance* is a vessel specially designed to hold the Blessed Sacrament for placement on an altar for times of worship and prayer or for use in a Eucharistic procession. It is often made of precious metal with a base, a stem, and a round top that encloses the Blessed Sacrament in glass for viewing.

14. Alternative Opening Prayer for the Solemnity of the Most Sacred Heart of Jesus.
15. *Lumen Gentium,* 59.
16. See the discussion of the Immaculate Conception below.
17. That is, formally recognized by the Church as being in heaven. This pronouncement is made only after a thorough investigation of the person to be canonized.
18. From the Preface of Christ the King.
19. From the Constitution *Ineffabilis Deus,* issued December 8, 1854.

Three
Sacramentals and Signs

1. CCC 2132.
2. From "Order for the Blessing of Images of the Saints," copyright 1987 by the International Committee on English in the Liturgy (ICEL).
3. *Instruction Concerning Worship of the Eucharistic Mystery,* 26, issued by the Sacred Congregation for the Sacraments and Divine Worship, April 17, 1980.
4. From "Order for the Blessing of Articles for Liturgical Use," copyright 1987 by ICEL.
5. From "Order for the Blessing of Religious Articles," copyright 1987 by ICEL.
6. Reliquaries are ornate containers that hold relics.
7. See the entry on "Candles" in *The Catholic Encyclopedia,* available online at www.newadvent.org/cathen.
8. See the Apostles' Creed.

Four
Patterns of Prayer

1. Vocal prayer can be silent as well. For example, saying the rosary quietly while engaged in other activity is more vocal prayer than mental prayer.
2. Pope John Paul II, apostolic letter "On Keeping the Lord's Day Holy" (*Dies Domini*), 52 (May 31, 1998).
3. Bishops' Committee on the Liturgy, United States Catholic Conference, *Music in Catholic Worship*, I.4 (1972).
4. *Music in Catholic Worship*, III.38.
5. *Music in Catholic Worship*, IV.54.
6. See Irenaeus, *Against Heresies*, V, 19.
7. CCC 2683.
8. CCC 2683.
9. St. Jerome, *Against Vigilantius*, 23.
10. Pope Paul VI, apostolic constitution *Indulgentiarum Doctrina*, Norm 1; see CCC 1471-79.
11. From the General Audience Address of Pope John Paul II on Wednesday, September 29, 1999.
12. *Enchiridion Indulgentiarum*, 66, 13, 29, 34, 30.
13. From the General Audience Address of Pope John Paul II on Wednesday, September 29, 1999.

Five
Trends and Developments

1. *Constitution on the Sacred Liturgy* (*Sacrosanctum Concilium*), 23.
2. *Sacrosanctum Concilium*, 23.
3. John Paul II, Address to the Bishops of the Antilles, May 8, 2002.

Further Reading

GENERAL

Catechism of the Catholic Church. 2d ed. Vatican City: Libreria Editrice Vaticana, 1997.

McBride, Alfred M. *Catholic Beliefs From A to Z: An Inspirational Dictionary.* Ann Arbor, Mich.: Servant, 2001.

Thigpen, Paul, and Leisa Thigpen. *Building Catholic Family Traditions.* Huntington, Ind.: Our Sunday Visitor, 1999.

SACRAMENTS

Ghezzi, Bert. *50 Ways to Tap the Power of the Sacraments.* Huntington, Ind.: Our Sunday Visitor, 1995.

Santa, Thomas M. *The Essential Catholic Handbook of the Sacraments: A Summary of Beliefs, Rites, and Prayers.* St. Louis, Mo.: Liguori, 2001.

Stravinskas, Peter. *Understanding the Sacraments: A Guide for Prayer and Study.* Ann Arbor, Mich.: Servant, 1989.

LITURGY

Aquilina, Mike. *The Mass of the Early Christians.* Huntington, Ind.: Our Sunday Visitor, 2001.

Fushek, Dale, and Bill Dodds. *Your One-Stop Guide to the Mass.* Ann Arbor, Mich.: Servant, 2000.

Lang, Jovian P. *Dictionary of the Liturgy.* Totowa, N.J.: Catholic Book Publishing, 1989.

Ratzinger, Joseph Cardinal. *Spirit of the Liturgy.* John Sward, Trans. San Francisco: Ignatius, 2000.

Socias, James. *Daily Roman Missal.* Huntington, Ind.: Our Sunday Visitor, 1994.

SACRAMENTALS

Aquilina, Mike, and Regis J. Flaherty. *The How-To Book of Catholic Devotions: Everything You Need to Know But No One Ever Taught You.* Huntington, Ind.: Our Sunday Visitor, 2000.

Chervin, Ronda De Sola, and Carla Conley. *The Book of Catholic Customs and Traditions: Enhancing Holidays, Special Occasions, & Family Celebrations.* Ann Arbor, Mich.: Servant, 1994.

DEVOTIONS

Aquilina, Mike, and Regis J. Flaherty. *The How-To Book of Catholic Devotions: Everything You Need to Know But No One Ever Taught You.* Huntington, Ind.: Our Sunday Visitor, 2000.

Dodds, Bill. *Your One-Stop Guide to How Saints Are Made.* Ann Arbor, Mich.: Servant, 2001.

Thigpen, Paul. *Jesus, We Adore You: Prayers Before the Blessed Sacrament.* Ann Arbor, Mich.: Servant, 2001.

NEW DEVELOPMENTS

Michalenko, Sophia. *The Life of Faustina Kowalska: The Authorized Biography.* Ann Arbor, Mich.: Servant, 1999.

Treece, Patricia. *Meet Padre Pio: Beloved Mystic, Miracle-Worker, and Spiritual Guide.* Ann Arbor, Mich.: Servant, 2001.